BEN COMEE
A TRUE TALE OF ROGERS'S RANGERS
1758 – 1759

BY M. J. CANAVAN

Introduction © 2020 by Brace E. Barber

Except for the Introduction, this work is in the public domain.

THIS SECTION FOR REFERENCE ONLY

Original Publishing and Copyright Notice.
New York
THE MACMILLAN COMPANY
LONDON: MACMILLAN AND CO., Ltd.
1922

Copyright, 1899,
By THE MACMILLAN COMPANY.

Set up and electrotyped October, 1899. Reprinted November, 1899; February, 1908; October, 1910; September, 1913; November, 1916.

Norwood Press
J. S. Cushing & Co.—Berwick & Smith
Norwood Mass. U.S.A.

Introduction 5
Contentment of a Life Well Lived..5
Large Map of Region with Modern Boundaries.........................11
1750s Large Map of Region 12
Map of Ben's Home and Battles 13
Chapter I: Ben Is Born in Lexington 1737—Schools and
Schoolfellows 16
Chapter II: They Trap Muskrats—Bishop Hancock and His
Grandson John...24
Chapter III: In Which are Details of a Great Fox Hunt..............34
Chapter IV: Trading in Those Days—Ben is Apprenticed—The
Enlisting Sergeant—Court Day at Concord 47
Chapter V: Pigeon Tuesday and its Exploits..............................55
Chapter VI: A Pauper's Funeral—Ben's Friend the Minister, and
Ben's Victory in Wrestling..61
Chapter VII: Tales From the Frontier—Mr. Tithingman and His
Services 70
Chapter VIII: Ben and Amos Join Rogers's Rangers and March to
the West 78
Chapter IX: In Which the Rangers Engage With the French and
Indians 84
Chapter X: Lord Howe and His Death—The Loyalty of John Stark
....90
Chapter XI: Fort Ticonderoga and the Assault...........................98
Chapter XII: The Fight at Fort Anne, and the Escape of Amos 105
Chapter XIII: Ben Comee Heap Big Paleface—Trapping Bobcats
in Primeval Woods 118
Chapter XIV: A Scouting Expedition in the Dead of Winter...133
Chapter XV: Camp Discipline—Amherst's Angels—A Brush with
the French, and the Loss of Captain Jacob 140
Chapter XVI: The Rangers to the Front—Captain Stark's Tale of
Capture—To Attack the St. Francis Indians.............................148
Chapter XVII: March to the Village—The Retreat..................159
Chapter XVIII: Starvation—Drifting Down the Ammonusuc—
Fort No. 4, and Good Fortune at Last.......................................170

Introduction

Contentment of a Life Well Lived

One of Ben Comee's childhood friends always had an elevated opinion of himself. Decades later, after the French and Indian, and Revolutionary Wars when Ben visited him, he was the Governor of Massachusetts, the richest man in Boston one of the top heroes of the American Revolution. Despite the elevated position of John Hancock, and his condescending attitude, Ben treated him like a regular man. Ben explains, "I saw no reason why I should look up to and revere him. I had played my own part in life well and boldly and stood firm on my feet." I know of no person who would not wish to truly think this about themselves in their inner thoughts as they aged. But how could Ben say that after the life that he had lived?

Ben Comee is a fascinating person because of the paradoxes that somehow peacefully existed within his character. Ben was a Christian who grew up in a world accepting of slavery and at war with the "redskins." Ben Comee described himself as a religious man, but he was described by another as, "A kind of mixture of bear, wildcat, and greased lightning." He served in Roger's Rangers with some of the most base and brutal men alive. Even among those men, Ben stood out as an exceptionally fierce fighter. The battles in which he participated necessitated his killing of men with rifles, axes and with his bare hands. He was so hated among the enemy that his scalp was as valued as Roger's and Stark's. Yet in the end, Ben was comfortable with how he had lived life.

Considering the society in which Ben grew up and lived, I believe that a Christian lens is the most accurate way to look at his life. Today's American Christian Church rarely produces people who can relate to the seriousness with which an 18th Century Colonial Christian took his faith. He was taught and took seriously humility, responsibility and obedience in line with Scripture. There is no indication that he ever cooled his beliefs, yet he was a first-rate combat killer. Ben never comes out and justifies his actions in battle, but through his impressions and thoughts, his mindset is revealed. He has an odd reaction in contemplation of one of the men that he had to kill in hand to hand combat. Later, as his unit is moving in for a surprise raid, he makes known his strange war-time desire for a fair fight.

Ben reconciled his beliefs with his actions so that later in life he was at peace with how he had lived. Ben's statement was based on his confidence in the truth of the values by which he lived. No one can claim to have played his part in life *well* unless he knows what well is and what ill is. He has to know the standard by which he is judged.

I recall in my years prior to becoming a Christian that I dragged along a nagging feeling that I had no idea what right and wrong were. In spite of the lack of definition, I was somehow confident that I was a good person. I believed that I was so good in fact that if I messed up a little bit here and there, I still had plenty of margin to give and still be good. When there is no definition of right and wrong we can only guess if we've been good. I knew that. I know now, much later in life, that if I had continued down that path, I would put on a good show of righteousness, but would be unable to confidently say to myself that I had lived life well.

Ben was able to have that peace and assurance that all of us desire. How, after his years of battle for a country that was forcibly moving Native American's from their homes and enslaving Africans, can a man have peace? We ask that now in a country that has murdered almost 50,000,000 children since 1970. We are born into our cultures and our times. None of us deserves to be judged based on the worst part of our societies. Our private judgements on ourselves are based on how well we live in accordance with our beliefs. We do not know what Ben's actions were with regard to slavery, but we do know that he fought both with and against Native Americans.

Was it wrong to kill Native Americans? Ben was born into a society fighting to survive against the ruthless and barbaric attacks of Native Americans. He inherited the battle. Was it wrong for the Native Americans to fight as they did? Was it wrong for Ben to fight on behalf of his country? Was it wrong for Ben to fight on behalf of his family and community?

I believe Ben was able to have peace because of his faith in the truth of Scripture. He knew how God helps people and how He judges people.

Ben surely noticed how grand John Hancock's home and furnishings were. Certainly there were servants and the best of food. We know that John applied pressure on Ben by expecting the reverence due to someone with his high position and heroic past. Yet Ben knows that,

> *"God does not show favoritism, but accepts from every nation the one who fears him and does what is right." – Acts 10:34-35.*

This is sometimes written, *God is no respecter of persons*. Many of us today wouldn't be able to contain our gushing respect if we found ourselves as the house guest of a highly-placed political figure. Or worse, we wouldn't be able to control ourselves if we were having lunch with a successful sports figure or actor. Ben knew that his value was not based on his income and refused to be impressed with the excess of others.

Ben's comments showed another aspect of his satisfaction with his life and his scriptural focus. Instead of being envious of his friend, he was content. Paul writes,

> *"I have learned the secret of being content in any and every situation, whether well fed or hungry, whether living in plenty or in want. I can do all this through him who gives me strength." –* Philippians 4:12-13

I think that Christians often misunderstand this scripture. We recite this verse when coming upon a difficult challenge to mean I can do or overcome anything, and maybe it is appropriate, but what it really shows is how horribly difficult it is to simply be content.

Americans are bred to be discontent. We must have more, better, faster, newer – now. We try to create contentment by buying things. Unfortunately, when combined with the nagging of not knowing the true boundaries of right and wrong, we find that the accumulation of things does not create contentment. Depression follows. Ben, however, was content. He was a man of his times who "played *his* own part in life well and boldly and stood firm on *his* feet." While John Hancock signed his commitment, Ben made it count by inflicting death on the enemy in horribly personal and brutal ways. They each played their part.

Ben knew the most important thing that his faith gave him – Forgiveness. Whether he was right or wrong to fight and kill Native Americans, forgiveness was available to him through the sacrifice of Jesus Christ. With repentance comes forgiveness. With forgiveness comes peace. Ben had peace and he had hope in eternity. With hope comes contentment no matter the circumstances. Ben knew that,

> *"Because of his great love for us, God, who is rich in mercy, made us alive with Christ even when we were dead in transgressions—it is by grace you have been saved." – Ephesians 2:4-5*

None of us are perfect. We all know that. How good do you have to be to say to yourself that you lived life well? By what standard are you judging good from evil?

We should desire to learn from the principles by which Ben Comee lived and which gave him contentment in his old age. How can we as individuals gain more peace within ourselves and with others? In a society of partisanship, how do we exist without throwing punches? How can we protect ourselves from the stress and anxiety of the constant argument? I'd suggest the principles of fearing God and doing what is right, finding contentment through Jesus Christ, and accepting the grace of salvation that God has offered. When you have hope in eternity, which I believe Ben had, you have the ability to be truly content.

This is a story of growing up in a caring family and transitioning to the army. Not 'the regulars' but the Rangers. This is the story like many young men today who grow up and ultimately serve as Army Rangers. What is hidden underneath the story of a country boy hunting and learning to be a blacksmith is the essence of the quiet professional. He was a man who kept his exceptional abilities to himself. Even after success, he was counselled by his dad to maintain his humility.

This is a full rounded story of a man who engaged in combat with vigor and success, but would rather tell a story about hunting. He would rather listen to the experiences of others than present his own story. You will find Ben Comee to be a man of substance and someone you'll enjoy getting to know in the following pages.

Large Map of Region with Modern Boundaries

Ben Comee; *A True Tale of Rogers's Rangers* 1758-59

1750s Large Map of Region

Map of Ben's Home and Battles

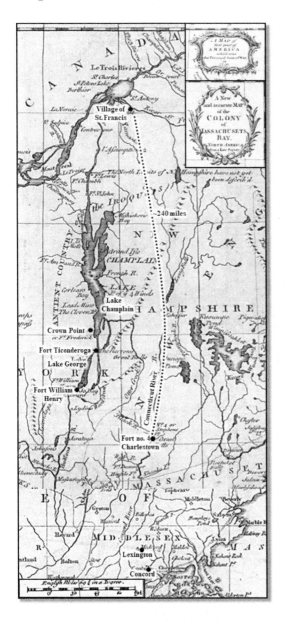

Ben Comee; *A True Tale of Rogers's Rangers* 1758-59

Chapter I: Ben Is Born in Lexington 1737—Schools and Schoolfellows

If you have occasion to pass through or to visit Lexington, be sure to put up at the tavern about a mile below Lexington Common on a little knoll near the main road.

In front of it stand two large elms, from one of which hangs the tavern sign. It is the best tavern in the place. You will find there good beds, good food, and a genial host. The landlord is my cousin, Colonel William Munroe, a younger brother of my old friend Edmund.

Sit with him under the trees. William will gladly tell you of the fight. Lord Percy's reinforcements met the retreating British soldiers near the tavern. Percy and Pitcairn had a consultation in the bar-room over some grog, which John Raymond mixed for them, for John took care of the tavern that day. After they departed, the soldiers entered and helped themselves freely to liquor from the barrels in the shop. Some of their officers knocked the spigots from the barrels and let the liquor run away on the floor. The drunken soldiers became furious. They fired off their guns in the house. You can still see a bullet hole in the ceiling.

William will show you the doorway where poor John Raymond, the cripple, was shot down by the soldiers, as he was trying to escape from the bar-room, and will point out the places nearby, where houses were burned by the British. And as you sit with William under the trees you will see great six or eight horse teams, laden with goods from New Hampshire, lumber along heavily over the road. Stages from Keene, Leominster, Lunenburg, and other towns will dash up to the door and passengers will alight for their meals. On Saturdays and Sundays herds of cattle are driven through on their way to the Brighton cattle market. All is bustle and activity.

Lexington in Early Times

I was born in this old house in the year 1737. In my boyhood Lexington was a dull little village unknown to fame. But the 19th of April, 1775, made the world familiar with the name. And since the bridges, which were built over the Charles River a few years later, placed the town on the main highway between Boston and the Back Country, it is now, in this year 1812, one of the most thriving places in the county.

In my childhood we were remote from the main travelled roads. The Back Country hardly existed. People were just beginning to settle the southern part of New Hampshire, and were in constant fear of Indians. Their time was fully occupied in cutting down the forests, fighting the redskins, and raising a scanty crop for their own support. Occasionally a fur trader, driving a pack horse laden with furs, passed through the town. The huts and log houses of the first settlers were still standing, and some of the people kept up an acquaintance and correspondence with their relatives in the old country.

My grandfather used to take me on his knee and tell me of events which happened far back in the seventeenth century. His father was a Highland lad, and during the wars between King Charles and Cromwell fought for the king in a regiment of Scotch Highlanders. At the battle of Dunbar the king's army was defeated, and several thousand Scotch soldiers were taken prisoners. Among them was my great-grandfather, David McComee.

In a few days they were drawn up in a line, and each man was tied to his neighbor by stout cords around their wrists. A guard of soldiers was put over them, and they were marched to Plymouth.

There they learned that they were to be sent to the colonies, as slaves or servants, with the right to buy back their freedom.

David Comee, The Redemptioner

David McComee and some two hundred and seventy other prisoners were packed on board the ship *John and Sara*; and after a long voyage arrived at Charlestown, where they were sold at auction. David's master lived in Woburn, near Lexington, or, as it was then called, Cambridge Fields. He was treated in a kindly manner. A little piece of land was given him, on which he built a hut. He worked for his master on alternate days. The rest of the time was his own. In a few years David McComee had earned enough to pay back the price of his purchase money, and was no longer a redemptioner, (*Someone who gained passage to America by becoming an indentured servant*) but a free man and his own master. By this time, he was known as David Comee. He moved to Concord, and as he was a thrifty, hard-working man, before long he was the owner of a snug little farm.

In 1675 the terrible war with King Philip broke out. The Indians ravaged the land, and boasted that no white man should dare to so much as poke his nose out of his house. We had then but a little fringe of settlements extending a few miles back from the coast. Concord was on the frontier. Word came that the neighboring town of Sudbury was attacked, and David Comee and ten companions started out to help the inhabitants.

My grandfather, who was then a small boy, said that after buckling on his iron breast and back plates, his father knelt with the family and prayed. Then he arose, kissed his wife and children, put on his steel cap, and taking his long firelock, started off to join the other men.

That afternoon they were lured into an ambush by the Indians, and most of them were killed. Reinforcements were sent to Sudbury. The Indians were driven off; and the next day David Comee was found lying in the water of the river meadow, scalped, and stripped of his armor and clothes.

Another Scotch redemptioner, named William Munroe, who was shipped to this country in the *John and Sara*, settled at Cambridge Fields or Lexington. My grandfather married his daughter Martha, and bought the place where my Cousin William now keeps the tavern.

Our family had no love for Indians. We hated them bitterly. At the present day, as we sit in our homes safe and without fear, we are apt to forget the constant dread in which the colonists lived. From 1690 until the end of the French war in 1763, few years passed in which the men on the frontier were not fighting the redskins.

Ben's Uncle John Killed

In 1707 my Uncle John went "to the Eastward" in a company of soldiers to help drive off a body of French and Indians from the settlements in Maine. He was killed there in a fight near the town of York.

He was my grandfather's eldest son, just arrived at manhood. I was a small boy when grandfather died; but I can remember how he straightened up, and a fierce fire came in his eyes, when the talk was of Indians. He was a strict member of the church, and never swore, but on these occasions he made use of some Old

Testament phrases and expressions which, I thought, answered the purpose very well.

You may pride yourself on your Latin and your Greek. I never got so far in my schooling. But turn this book upside down and read it. You cannot and I can.

I might have become quite a scholar, if I had been properly brought up, for I learned to do this at Millicent Mason's elementary school before I was six years old.

She sat in a chair and held a book in her lap. We stood in front of her. She would point out the letters with her knitting-needle and ask, "What is that letter? And that? And that?" Then she would ask us what the word was. In this way, we learned our A B C's. Then one-syllable, and two-syllable words, and finally to read a book held upside down. I can do it now; and occasionally, if I find a friend reading, I surprise him by glancing over the top of the page and repeating a few lines of the text.

As I grew older, I went to the man's school and learned to read in the ordinary way. It was kept in a little old schoolhouse about twenty feet square, which stood on a knoll on the common. There was a great fireplace at one end of it; and the teacher sat in a great chair on a platform, with a table in front of him. We paid two pence a week for being taught reading, and three pence a week for "righting and siphering," as the town clerk entered it on his books.

Lexington Common

Our teachers were young men just out of college, and the one who would serve for the smallest pay was the one always chosen. We had a new teacher every year.

At the lower end of the common was the old ramshackle meeting house, facing down the road.

In front of the meeting house were a couple of horse-blocks, on which the women dismounted as they rode to meeting on their pillions, behind their husbands or brothers.

On either side of the door were tacked up notices of public auctions, lotteries, public proclamations, and the appointment of administrators. Between the school and the meeting house were two pairs of stocks, in which we occasionally found some offender seated with his feet sticking out through the holes.

On the opening day of school, there was a man in each of them. One was a man who obstinately refused to go to meeting, and after being warned several times was clapped into the bilboes *(iron restraints normally placed on a person's ankles)* by the tithingman *(peace officer)*. The other was some poor vagrant who had tried to settle in the town, but because he was needy and shiftless he had been warned out, and as he did not go, was put in the stocks.

The school children gathered about them, seated on the hard boards, with their feet sticking out through the holes in the stocks, and discussed their crimes and punishment, and made bets as to the number of nails in the soles of their shoes. William Munroe, the blacksmith, came over from his shop with his leather apron on.

"Come, Sam, you want to get out of there, and sit in the seats with the righteous. It's never too late for the sinner to repent."

"Oh, go away, Bill. Let me alone. It's bad enough to sit here in these cussed stocks, until every bone in my body aches, and have the children stare at me, without you coming over to poke fun at me. I'm sick of it."

"That's right! A change of heart will do you good. See you in meeting next Sabbath."

The next day, Robert Harrington, the constable, drove up to the stocks with his cart.

"See here, Bob. Let me out. I give in. I'll go to meeting twice a day for the fifty-two Sabbaths in the year, and on lecture days and any other days that they want me to go."

Vagrants and Sinners

"All right; I'll let you out, but they will expect an acknowledgment from you of your wrongdoing, in meeting next Sabbath."

"Just let me out of these stocks, and I'll do anything they ask."

Mr. Harrington released him, and then turned to the vagrant and said, "Come, old boy, you've got to move on. We can't have you on our hands."

He took him in his cart, carried him miles away, and dumped him in the road, just as you would an old cat that you wanted to get rid of; and warned him never to come back.

Next Sabbath the sinner made a "public relation" before the meeting, in which he confessed his grievous sins and promised to amend.

My greatest friend was my cousin, Edmund Munroe, a sturdy, trustworthy boy with great common sense.

Then there was Davy Fiske, a son of Dr. Fiske. Davy was a lean, wiry fellow, not much of a boy for study, but full of knowledge of the woods. He knew when every kind of bird came and departed. Could tell you the best place to hunt foxes. He knew what they would do and where they would go. If a wolf had been killed, Davy could give the whole story. If a bear had carried off a pig or a sheep, Davy would go miles to be one of the party to follow him up.

It must be admitted that, like many other hunters, Davy had imagination, and did not allow dull facts to hem him in when he told a hunting story.

Edmund used to take his lunches with his cousin, William Munroe, the blacksmith, whose house and shop were just below the common. I generally brought my lunch to school in a basket, and ate it in the school at noon time. After lunch, we would prowl about and explore. We used to climb the stone wall of the pound, and look into it, to see what stray cattle might be there; and wandered down Malt Lane to John Munroe's malt house and watched him change the barley into malt, and looked at the hams and sides of bacon that the people had brought to be smoked.

The Blacksmith's Shop

The most interesting place to us was the blacksmith's shop. If an ox was brought in to be shod, they drove him into a stall and fastened his head in the stanchions at the end of it. A broad sheet of canvas hung down on one side of the stall, and they pulled the free end of it under the belly of the ox, and fastened it by hooks to a windlass on the other side of the stall, about the height of one's head. William Munroe and his son Will took a few turns at the windlass, and the ox would be lifted off his feet. The sides of the stall were only eighteen inches high, and were of thick plank, with a groove in the top edge. They bent up the leg of the ox and rested his cloven hoof in the groove, and shod each part with a piece of iron.

But beside shoeing horses and oxen, the blacksmith made all kinds of implements, andirons, latches and hinges for doors. They fastened an iron edge to wooden shovels, and made chains and nails.

Chapter II: They Trap Muskrats—Bishop Hancock and His Grandson John

One day while we were pulling over a lot of old truck in a corner of the shop, we found some rusty muskrat traps. Edmund asked William if he used them. "No; I did considerable trapping when I was a boy. You and Ben may have them if you want them. Your father and I trapped together one winter; and we used to go hunting wild turkeys too. There were a number of them over at Mt. Gilboa and Turkey Hill. They're pretty much all gone now. We had lots of fun with these traps, and I hope you boys will."

There were fourteen traps. We greased them up and put them in good condition. And one Saturday early in the fall we got Davy to go with us to the great meadows and look the ground over. Davy said, "We must find their paths." When we found one, we looked for the best place to set a trap. "Now, see here. Here's a place where they come out of the water; and they climb up on that old root. Take the axe, Ben, and cut a notch in it a little under the water; and I'll smear the notch with mud so that the rat won't notice it."

Trapping Muskrats

We opened the trap, and set it in the notch; and then fastened the chain, which was attached to the trap, to a stick; and drove the stick into the bank a little way up the stream. "Let's put the next trap in the path. Drive the stick into the ground, so that they can't carry the trap off. That's right. Now set the trap and sprinkle some leaves over it to hide it."

In some of the brooks we drove a couple of sticks into the bank, so that the trap would rest on them, a couple of inches beneath the surface of the water, and fastened the chain up stream. We drove a stick into the bank about ten inches above the trap, and stuck a sweet apple on the end of it. "There, that looks real tempting. A rat will come swimming along, and when he sees that apple, he will jump for it; and if you are lucky, he will fall into the trap."

"Who's that over on the island in the meadow?"

"Captain Wooton. He's girdling *(removing bark from around a section of a tree)* trees."

"What's he doing that for?"

"To kill them off. That's the way the Indians cleared their land. The trees die, and when they are dead, he sets them on fire in the wet season, and burns them up. He was a sea captain, and married one of the Winship girls, and old Mr. Winship gave them this land."

"Well, let's hurry up and set the rest of the traps. I've got to get home to my chores."

Edmund lived on the further side of the meadows and close to them, and in going to school passed several brooks that flowed into them. I lived above the meadows, and had to go out of my way to reach them. So Edmund looked after nine traps, and I took care of five. Every morning we examined the traps, to see if we had caught anything, and to set them again, and bait them. If a trap was not in sight, we pulled on the chain, and generally found a muskrat in the trap, drowned, with his hair all soaked down on his sides. Sometimes we would find one alive in a trap in their paths, and sometimes only a foot.

David's Black Cat

Occasionally my little brother David went with me, and while I was baiting a trap, would run on, to see if there was anything in the next one. Once he came back to me, and said, "Benny, some mean fellow has been down here, and stuck a nasty black cat in the trap." The cat turned out to be a mink with a fine fur. After we had examined the traps, Edmund and I used to meet at a spot on Deacon Brown's farm, which was so pretty that folks called it "God's Creation"; and then we went over to the highway together, on our way to school.

We trapped muskrats until April, and got fifty-four muskrats and two mink. Skins are like oysters, good every month in the year that has an *R* in it.

How many were actually caught in our traps is another matter. A half-breed Indian named Tony lived in a little hut by the edge of the meadows. Frequently we found prints of his moccasins by our traps; and they would be baited with a different kind of an apple from that we used.

Probably Tony needed muskrat skins more than we, or at least thought that he did.

We disliked Tony and avoided him. We had our little scalping parties or war paths and ambushes, in imitation of the Indians, but in spite of that we hated them heartily, and thought it a great weakness on the part of our minister, Bishop Hancock, when he spoke a good word for them.

Bishop Hancock

He, Bishop Hancock, was of the salt of the earth. He was very old, but bright and strong, and as full of fun as a kitten. Old age seemed to improve him, as it does wine, and made him ripe and mellow.

When we saw him walking down the road, with his full-bottomed white wig, his black coat and small clothes, his black silk stockings, and his white Geneva bands, we gathered on one side of the road, folded our hands, ducked our heads, and made our manners.

He always had some funny or quaint remark to make to us. There was, perhaps, nothing wonderful in what he said, but his words always had a pleasant savour; and the day seemed brighter after he had spoken to us. He was himself like one of those serene peaceful days that come in the Indian summer near the close of the year.

He had so much common sense and so sure a judgment that all the ministers of the county ran to him for advice, if any important matter came up. And he had such authority among them, that they called him Bishop Hancock, for he was as a bishop to them; and they loved and revered him as much as they would have hated a real bishop.

His grandson, John Hancock, came to live with him, and went to school with us. Young John was of our age, bright, quick-witted, with a kind heart, an open hand, and a full allowance of self-conceit.

He was always boasting about his Uncle Thomas, the richest man in Boston, of his wharf and warehouses and ships, and of his new stone house on the Beacon Hill.

"And after I go to college, I'm going to live with Uncle Thomas, and be a merchant like him," he used to proclaim.

Edmund, Davy, and I went up to Bishop Hancock's one noon with John, and made a careful and minute survey of the premises, after the manner of boys. We inspected the pigs beneath the barn, and got a pail of water and scrubbed them with a broom until we were satisfied with their appearance. Then we learned the names and good points of the cows and horses. When we got to the loft,

Davy made a great discovery—a pigeon net stowed away on the rafters. Before we left, John had obtained a promise from his grandfather that he might use it to catch pigeons.

The next day we took it to a hill on the other side of the road, and looked for a place to spread it. John knew as much about pigeon catching as a hen does about skating. But he ordered us about, right and left, until Davy objected.

"See here, John! That place you chose is full of humps and hollows, and won't do. We want a level spot, where the net will lie flat; and we must have a good place nearby, where we can hide. What's the matter with that open place over there, with the big clump of bushes behind it?"

They Set a Pigeon Net

"Well, I guess that's all right."

"Now, boys," said Davy, "peg down one end of the net. That's it. Spread it out. It lies like a tablecloth on a table. Fold it up, so that the pole will be on top. Now fasten the springs into the ground. Set them and rest the pole on them. Fasten the strings to each spring, so that when we pull, the springs will fly up, and throw the pole forward over the pigeons. That's right. Now let's try it."

We went back toward the bushes and pulled the strings. The springs threw the pole forward, and the net was spread out on the ground.

"How soon can we begin, Davy?" asked John.

"Not for three or four days. We'll fold the net up and set it; and you must come up here every evening and bait the ground by throwing down some grain. When the birds get used to the net, we can come up and catch them."

John reported to us daily that the birds were getting tamer, and were not afraid of the net.

On Saturday we went up and hid in the bushes. John held the strings of course. We could see the pigeons picking up the grain, and when a number were together, Davy said "Now, John!"

John pulled the strings, and the pole was thrown forward so that the net fell over the pigeons. We rushed up and stood on the edge of the net. As the pigeons poked their heads up through the meshes, we wrung their necks.

We set the net three times and caught a couple of dozen of pigeons. Then we went to the house, and John told of the pigeons he had caught.

"Didn't the other boys have anything to do with it?"

"Oh, yes, they helped, but I pulled the strings."

Bishop Hancock's Dressing Gown

"I've noticed that it isn't always the man that pulls the strings who does the real solid work," said Mr. Hancock.

We did not have many quarrels or lawsuits in his time. If any dispute arose, he interfered, heard both sides, and settled the case. His decision ended the matter, for the defeated person knew that everyone in town would stand by Bishop Hancock's law.

I was playing in the yard with John one afternoon, when Mr. Hancock came to the window. He had on a gorgeous flowered silk dressing gown, and instead of his big white wig, wore on his head a cap or turban of the same gorgeous silk. I hardly knew him, and stared at him.

"What's the matter, Benny? Oh, it's the dressing gown and cap. You probably took me for some strange East India bird—a peacock, perhaps. It's nothing but some finery my son Thomas sent me to put on in the house. After wearing black all my life, it is very pleasant to move through the rooms looking like a rainbow."

"You did kind of startle me, sir. I suppose Joseph's coat must have looked a good deal like that."

"Ha, ha, Benny, I guess you're right. And it aroused envy. Mrs. Hancock said yesterday that this would make a fine gown. I must be careful to whom I show myself in this attire.

"I hear that there is a quarrel between Sam Locke and Jesse Robinson over the boundary line between their farms up on the old Salem road.

"I want you to go up there, John, and tell them that I wish both of them to meet me at the boundary line tomorrow afternoon at five o'clock. You might go with him, Benny, if you have time."

We did our errand, and the two men, in rather a surly manner, promised to meet Mr. Hancock. The next afternoon Mr. Hancock gave us a couple of stakes, which he told us to sharpen, and then we went up to the Salem road together. We found Sam and Jesse sitting on a stone wall, waiting.

Mr. Hancock said, "Well, neighbors, I hear that you have a dispute over your boundaries, and that you're going to law about it. That won't do at all. I'm not going to have you spending your money fighting this matter in one court and then in another, until your money is gone. We can clear up the trouble here today. State your cases to me, and I can give as good a decision as any court. Go on, Sam, and tell your story. Wait until he's through, Jesse, before you say a word." Sam told his side of the case, and then Jesse, and then Sam had a second chance, and after him Jesse again.

Bishop Hancock's Law

Though Sam and Jesse were supposed to do all the talking, yet the bishop had his say, too. And he was so sensible and genial that soon there was a different feeling between the two men. He told stories of their fathers when they were boys; what great friends they were, and how they bought adjoining farms to be near each other. "And as for that onion bed which marked the southern boundary of Jesse's farm, I have a very good idea of where it was. And probably we can see now where it was by the difference in the grass." He walked along and said, "A big stone with a flat top stuck up about twenty feet from the edge of the bed."

"Why, that's just ahead of us," said Jesse.

"I thought so. And now that I've heard your stories, and remember the onion bed and the stone, I think that this is the boundary line. Drive a stake down here, Benny. Now, neighbors, we've got it settled without costing a penny, and I want you to shake hands and be as close friends as your fathers were; for you're both good fellows."

How we did enjoy that old man! One day Edmund and John and I were seated in his yard, near the stable, mending the pigeon net, and Bishop Hancock was oiling a harness hanging just inside the barn, when the gate opened, and two old fools came into the yard.

"Good morning, Mr. Hancock."

"Good morning, neighbor Hall and neighbor Perry. You've caught me in a nice mess. There's nothing very ministerial about this. Quite different from preaching a long sermon at you; and to tell the truth, I half believe we preach too much. My friend Cotton Mather had a story of an old Indian who was in jail, about to be hanged for some crime.

Would-Be Elders

"A minister visited him in his cell and prayed with him and preached at him until the Indian begged the jailer to hurry up the hanging. He preferred it to any more talk.

"This harness was getting about as rusty as my old bones and needed oiling badly. And now, neighbors, is there anything I can do for you?"

"Well, Mr. Hancock, your remark just now about your age is to the point. Some years ago you had the help of your good son Ebenezer, whose loss we all deplore. And some of us have been considering your great age, and the numerous and hard duties you perform; and we have thought it might be well if you had some assistance and aid. We know that it used to be common to have a couple of elders to assist the pastor; and thought that you might find it pleasant to revive the office, and have the help of two elders."

Mr. Hancock thought for a moment and said, "That's an excellent notion. But where can we find men ready to fulfil the duties of the office?"

"Well, Uriah and me have been talking it over, and we would be willing to take the office, for the sake of helping you."

"I suppose you know the duties of elders?"

"No! But you know all about it, and could tell us."

"Well, gentlemen, the duties of elders have never been very clearly defined in the church. But latterly they have settled down to this. The younger elder is to brush down and harness the pastor's horse when he wishes to ride out, and the elder is to accompany him, when he goes out of town, and pay his bills. I should be glad to have you appointed."

Uriah gave a gasp, and said, "Hello! It looks as if there was a shower coming up, and my hay's out. Goodbye, Mr. Hancock; we'll see you another day."

The bishop looked after them, as they walked away, and turned round with a twinkle in his eye. Seeing us laughing, he laughed too, and said,—

No Elders in Mr. Hancock's Day

"I don't believe we shall have any elders in Lexington, boys. At least, not in my day."

Chapter III: In Which are Details of a Great Fox Hunt

When the winter came there were a great many quail about our barn. Smiling Bill Smith, who worked for us,—Old Bill Smiley some folks called him, on account of the broad grin he always wore,—said to me—

"Them whales, Ben, pretty near bother the life out of me. They creep in through the cracks and crannies and eat the grain. If I go over by the grain chest, the first thing I know, there's a whir, and a cloud of them darts up in front of my face. Sometimes it makes my heart come right up in my mouth. I wish there wasn't a whale round the place."

"Quails, Bill. What makes you call them whales?"

"Whales I heard them called when I was a boy, and whales they are to me."

Catching Quail

"Perhaps you think it was one of these whales that swallowed Jonah?"

"I never did think so, Benny. But if he did, it was a miracle, sure enough."

Davy helped me make a figure-4 trap to catch them. One Saturday morning I met Edmund down at John Buckman's store, trading some butter and eggs for tea and sugar.

"Come up to the house, Edmund. I've got a figure-4 trap; and we'll catch some quail."

We set the trap, and put some grain under the box. Several quail flew down, hopped about, and soon discovered the grain. While they were pecking away at it, they sprang the trap. The box fell over them, and we caught three.

"Now, Edmund, you find some grass seed in the barn, and sprinkle it in a line from the door. And I'll go and get the gun, and we'll take a raking shot at them."

I went after the gun, and gave it to him. We hid in the barn, and before long some more quail flew down and began to eat the seed. When they were well in line he fired, and killed four and wounded several. The wounded ones hopped about, cried out, and took on piteously, and acted like so many little children in distress.

I did not like this at all, and Edmund seemed very much troubled.

"Come on, Edmund. We've got to kill those that are sure to die. The rest we will put in a box with some hay, and perhaps they will get well."

We wrung the necks of three, and put the others in a box and covered it over.

Then we looked at each other, and Edmund opened his basket, and let those we had caught fly away.

"No more quail shooting for me, Ben. They're too human. By George, I know just how a murderer feels."

One snowy winter day, Davy came to our barn, where I was foddering the cattle, and said,—

"Ben, this storm will be over tomorrow, and will make fine snowshoeing. Amos Locke is going with me fox hunting, and we want you to come too."

Invitation to a Fox Hunt

"I don't know that I can go. Let's talk it over with my brother John."

When John heard us he said, "I guess I can fix things so that you can get off. Pitch in, work hard, and do some of the stints that father set you for tomorrow, and I will look after your chores."

By the time mother came to the door and blew the horn for supper, we had done a great deal of work.

After supper I lit a big pine knot and placed it in the side of the fireplace, so that the smoke from it would go up the chimney. It threw a pleasant light out into the room. Father was at work on an oxbow. John had a rake into which he was setting some new teeth, and I sat on a stool with a wooden shovel between my legs, shelling corn; rasping the ears on the iron edge of the shovel, so that the kernels fell into a big basket in front of me.

My little brother David was sitting on a bench in the side of the great fireplace, reading that terrible poem by the Rev. Michael Wigglesworth, called the "Day of Doom," which tells all about the day of judgment—how the sinners are doomed to burn eternally in brimstone; and the saints are represented as seated comfortably in their armchairs in heaven, looking down into the sulphurous pit.

I used to wonder how Mr. Wigglesworth got so thorough a knowledge of these two places and of judgment day, and doubts crept into my mind as to the accuracy of his description. When I thought of Bishop Hancock seated in one of those armchairs, I knew that his soul, at least, would be full of pity and sorrow for the poor sufferers below, and I felt that the saints ought to be a good deal like him.

I did not envy David his book. It seemed to me that every now and then I could see his hair rise up and his eyes bulge out with terror.

Mother stood by the woolen wheel, spinning, and my little sister Ruhama sat near her, knitting.

The fire lit up the room and made the pewter dishes on the dresser shine.

Above us, hanging from the rafters, were bunches of herbs, crooked-neck squashes, and poles on which were strung circular slices of pumpkin which were drying, to be made into sauce in the future.

The "Day of Doom"

David shut up his book, went to mother, and said, "Oh, mother, mother! I'm scared to death. Do you suppose I've got to go to hell?"

"No, David. You're a good little boy. Just learn your catechism, go to meeting, and be a good boy, and I guess you'll come out all right."

I remembered well how I felt as I read that book, and the hours of anguish that it caused me. David got some apples, placed them on the hearth in front of the fire; and, in watching them roast and sputter, he soon forgot his fears.

John began to talk to father about old times, and soon got him started telling stories about hunting.

"Yes, I used to go after wild turkeys with Will Munroe, the blacksmith, when I was a boy. One day we met Ben Wellington, and he said he had just come down the Back Road, and had seen a bear in a huckleberry patch, and if we'd go with him, we could kill him. He borrowed a gun of Tom Fessenden, and we drew our charges, and loaded with a bullet and some buckshot. When we got to the place, we crept along carefully, and saw the bear stripping off the huckleberries and eating them. He was so busy he didn't notice us, and we got quite close to him. Will and I fired, and he rose and turned to us, and Ben fired. We ran off a little, loaded again, and went back, and found the bear was dead.

"In the winter we used to go fox hunting. What fun we had! I'd like to go now."

This gave John a good opening, and he said, "Young David Fiske and Amos Locke are going after foxes tomorrow, and they want Ben to go with them. Benny worked hard today, and did most of the jobs that you laid out for him to do tomorrow; and I told him that if you would let him go, I would do his chores."

"Well," said father, "one can't be young but once in one's life. I certainly did have great fun hunting when I was a boy; and if you'll do Benny's chores, I think we can manage to let him go. But it was a pretty sly trick of yours, John, to lead the talk around to hunting, and get me worked up over it, before you said anything about tomorrow."

Luxurious Living

"I thought it would be a good idea to make you remember how much you liked it yourself."

The clock struck nine, and we got up and put our things away. Father read a chapter from the Bible. Then I raked up a great mass of red coals, and covered them carefully with ashes to keep them alive until the morning.

John and I went up to the attic, where we slept; and as I undressed and lay down in my straw bed, I could hear the wind hum and whistle as it caught on the roof, and cold draughts swept through the attic.

I pulled the blankets and comforter closely about me, and was soon asleep, dreaming of foxes.

When I awoke, I jumped out of bed and stepped into some snow that had sifted in through the cracks and formed a little drift over my leather breeches, which were frozen hard as a board. I shook the snow off them, and, grabbing up my clothes, ran downstairs, pulled the ashes off the coals, and fanned them until they were bright, and built a good fire in the fireplace. I warmed my leather breeches over the fire until they were softened so that I could get into them.

It was a little after five o'clock. The snowstorm was over, and the moon was shining bright.

Mother came in and said, "Well, Benny, you've built me a nice fire, and I hope you'll have a good time."

She hung a pot with some hasty pudding in it over the fire, warmed it up, and fried some pork in the skillet. I brought up a jug of cider from the cellar, and as I was eating breakfast, father came in and took down the gun from over the fireplace. "I think I'll put a new flint in the gun, Ben. You don't want to misfire when you get a chance to shoot at a fox. Be careful of the gun. You know it belonged to your Uncle John, and he had it with him when he was killed in the Indian fight up to York, the same time that Ben Muzzy was captured and carried off. I never take it down without thinking of John. He was dreadful fond of hunting, just as you be, Benny. You put me in mind of him."

Ben Starts for the Fox Hunt

I pulled some long stockings that belonged to my brother John over my own shoes and stockings, put on my woolen frock, and buckled my belt round my waist. Father handed me the gun, and said, "Give my respects to Dr. Fiske, Benny, and good luck to ye."

When I got outdoors, I slipped my toes under the thongs of the rackets, and shuffled along over the fields until I got to the road. The moon was bright, and everything was distinct and clear.

I skimmed along over the snow, and William Munroe, the blacksmith, came out of his house near the foot of the common, just as I was passing.

"Hello, Benny, you're up early today. Where are you bound for?"

"Fox hunting with Davy Fiske."

"Well, he's a good one at it, and it will be a fine day."

The meeting house was covered with a casing of snow. As I passed by the common I could see lights in Sam Jones's house and in old John Muzzy's. I kept on up the road by Jonas Parker's, and when I came in sight of Dr. Fiske's place, Davy was outside, waiting for me.

"Hello, Ben! Where have you been? I've been waiting for you these two hours."

"Oh, pshaw, Davy. This is plenty early. You can't see the least bit of daylight yet, and one can't do much with foxes until the sun is well up and warms the scent."

The doctor came to the door and said,—

"Don't mind David, Benny. You're early enough. But he's crazy about hunting, and wants to be at it all the time. It would be better for him if he spent less time at it."

"Father told me to give his respects to you, sir."

"All right, Benny. Now, boys, take things easy, or you'll be tired out before you see a fox."

Zabdiel

As Davy and I skimmed along over the snow, the day began to break. We had only one dog with us, but he was a real good one. His name was Zabdiel.

"That's a good dog, Davy, but he's got the funniest name for a dog I ever heard. How did he get it?"

"Oh, I dunno! Father gave it to him. There was a doctor in Boston started this inoculation business for the smallpox. Folks were about ready to tear his house down; but he kept on inoculating. His patients didn't die, and finally people let up on him. Father thinks a heap of this inoculation and sets a store by this Dr. Zabdiel Boylston, and named his best horse and dog after him."

"But I should think we ought to have more than one dog with us, Davy."

"Well, ain't we going over to Dog Lane, to pick up little Amos Locke? Every one over there hunts and has a dog. When we get there, you'll find Amos walking up and down, and all the dogs of Dog Lane following him. You won't be looking for dogs when you get there. The question will be, how to get rid of them."

Just then Davy held up his hand. "Hush, Ben," and pointed to a spot where the snow had been shaken up. "Give me a racket." I did so. He held it over the spot, and stuck his hand under it into the snow. Something darted up against the racket, and at the same time I was covered with snow from head to foot, and a partridge flew off. Davy laughed. "Why didn't you catch him, Ben? I got one." He drew his hand out with a partridge in it. He twisted its neck, and we started on again.

"The partridges dive down into the snow, and sleep there, but I don't see why those two went to bed so late after the storm was over. Something must have disturbed them. If I hadn't the racket to clap over the place, I should have lost him. I learned that trick from Amos Locke's father.

"But there is Amos, waiting for us, with all the dogs of Dog Lane about him. What did I tell you about dogs?"

"Isn't Amos rather young to go fox hunting, Davy?"

Amos Locke

"Sho! That's all you know about it. That little hatchet-faced fellow is tougher than a boiled owl, and knows almost as much about foxes and birds as I do, and that's saying a good deal. He's big too for his age, and will be pretty strong, though I don't suppose he will be as strong as you are. What do you do, Ben, to make you so strong? I could walk the legs off of you; but you've got a terrible grip, and throw me just as easy as nothing at all. If you keep on, you'll be as good a wrestler as Jonas Parker; and he's the best the whole country round. How do you get so strong?"

"Oh, I dunno! Father's strong, and mother's strong. Comes natural, I suppose."

"Well, perhaps so. Father's a doctor, and my brothers are going to be doctors; but I ain't. I'm going to be a hunter."

Amos shouted: "Hello, Dave and Ben! Where have you been? I'd about g-g-given you up." Amos stammered a little, except when he was stirred up, and then he stammered a good deal.

"Now, don't you get excited, sonny. We've got the whole day before us. Do you own all these dogs?"

"Oh, d-darn it, Davy, I can't help it. The whole pack of them keep following me all the time, and if I've got a gun, they stick to me like g-g-glue."

"Well! They're beauties. Regular full-blooded foxhounds, every one of them."

"Oh, get out, Dave. They may not be p-p-pretty, but they hunt almost as g-good as Zabdiel. Come here, Zab, old boy. I've been trying to get rid of them for the last two hours. But they seem to g-g-get out about as fast as I p-put them in."

"Well, come on over to Bear's Hill. That's the best place. Call your beauties in."

We kept on past Corner Hedge and Pine Grove until we came to Listening Hill. There the hounds struck a scent, lifted up their heads, bayed, and started off on the trail.

At first they went along the foot of Listening Hill, then up it, and over the top. We had to take our rackets off, for it was so rocky and uneven that we could not use them. The rocks stuck up through the snow. Holding our rackets under our left arms and our guns in our right hands, we followed over the crest of the hill, along the high land, and then down the slope. Here we put on our rackets again. The dogs were far ahead of us. We came to low land with a brook running through it, and in the distance could see the dogs.

Beaver Holes

"Hold on, boys," said Davy; "this won't do. That fox is too many for us." And putting his fingers to his mouth, he gave three shrill whistles. "That will call Zab back. It won't do for us to go fooling round on that swamp. It's full of holes, six to eight feet deep, that they call beaver holes. I don't know why; perhaps the beaver made them when they were here. If you get into one of them, it's all up with you, and the snow covers everything up so smooth that we can't tell where they are. That fox don't live here anyway, and is making straight for home, and he may live ten miles off.

"There's a nice spring of water in the side of Listening Hill. We'd better go over to it and have something to eat, and then we can start out again."

We went to the spring and had a good drink. Then we took out the food that our mothers had put up for us. We munched away, and before long Zab came back.

"I wonder where those other fool dogs are," said Davy.

"Oh, they're all right. They'll come to Dog Lane tonight all b-beat out, and they'll let me alone for a week."

"I tell you what it is," said Davy. "We ought never to have gone on that trail. We ought to have gone to Bear's Hill, just as we started to. There's always some foxes at Bear's Hill that live there, and don't want to leave home. Let's go after them."

After we had eaten our fill we threw the rest of our food on the snow, and Zab gulped it down in no time and had a contented look, probably thinking of those other dogs with their empty bellies.

We started off for Bear's Hill, and Davy said, "This is a different kind of a place. Foxes that you find here belong here."

The Fox Hunt

We came on a fox track, and Zab started off on it, and we after him. First we went along one side of the hill, then over it, and we had to take off our rackets again. Then along the foot of the hill, and Davy said, "He lives here. We'll get him. Pull off your frock, Ben." And he began to pull off his.

"Now, Amos, you go up that lane until you come to a gap in the hill. A stone wall crosses it, and almost always when you hunt round this hill, the fox comes down that gully to the stone wall. Get behind a bush near the wall; and you'll see the fox come down the hollow to it. And he will put his fore paws up on the wall, and wait a moment to hark for the dog. When he does that, you give it to him. Take our frocks, and if you feel cold, put one of them on. Wait there, and keep your eyes and ears open."

Amos went up the lane, and we followed Zab. At last he seemed to be coming somewhat toward us.

"Let's spread out a bit, Ben, and try to head the fox off."

He ran to the right, and I followed him, at some distance behind. We could hear that Zab was coming nearer, as we ran, and at last we heard a bang.

"The little cuss has got him, I'll bet you. Come on, Ben."

We ran on and came to the gully; and at the lower end of it was Amos, with my frock on, which reached down to the ground. He was holding up the fox, and Zab was jumping up and down.

"Good boy, Amos! Now tell us about it."

"Well, I did just as you t-t-told me, Davy. I went up the lane until I c-came to the gully and saw the stone wall. I found a good b-bush about twenty-five yards from the wall, and got behind it and waited until I began to feel c-cold. I pulled Ben's frock on, and left the neck of it open so that I could get the stock of the gun in to my shoulder, and spread out your f-frock and knelt on it. Then I heard Zab, and knew that he was c-coming toward me. I got ready and saw the fox creeping down the g-gully, and he did just as you said he would. When he got to the wall he p-put his fore paws upon it, p-pricked up his ears, and moved them forward and back as he listened for Zab, and I f-fired. I aimed at his b-b-breast and p-put two b-buckshot in his breast and one in his neck."

Dr. Fiske Has a Patient

"Yer done well, Amos. I couldn't a done better myself. He has a good fur and is a mighty fine fox."

It was getting pretty well along in the afternoon, and we thought we had had enough of hunting. I picked up the fox and carried it for Amos until we reached Dog Lane, when he left us. We found the partridge where we had tied it to a branch.

When we reached Dr. Fiske's, his sleigh was in front of the door. The doctor had put on a small riding wig with an eelskin cue, and was getting into his greatcoat.

"You're just in time, Benny; old Francis Whittemore, down at the East Village, has had a fit; and I've got to go and see what I can do for him. The old man has too much blood, and it's gone to his head. We must bleed him. Take the lancets, Jonathan, and the basin too, and a bottle of Daffy's Elixir. There's nothing like it to tone up the stomach. Now we are all ready. Tie your rackets on behind and sit in the bottom of the sleigh, Ben."

The doctor and his son Jonathan got in, and I sat in the straw until the doctor pulled up and let me out not far from our house.

Chapter IV: Trading in Those Days—Ben is Apprenticed—The Enlisting Sergeant—Court Day at Concord

About this time my life changed a good deal. Bishop Hancock had died during the previous winter. Young John was adopted by his Uncle Thomas, the Boston merchant, and went to Harvard College. Edmund's mother, who had been a widow several years, married Squire Bowman, and went to live at his house at the south end of the town. As for myself, I was growing up, and had my stint of work with the others. In the spring, driving the oxen, while father held the plough. Then came sowing the land and planting corn. Then half-hilling and again hilling it. Then helping to hay, and to gather in the crops. In the fall, picking apples and making cider. And as the winter came on, I helped to kill and dress a steer and a couple of hogs, and to put them in the powdering tubs and pickle them. Then we hung the hams and sides of bacon up in the chimney to be cured. Beside these things the daily care of the cattle and milking kept me busy all the time.

And it seemed to me that we got but small return for our labor. We had a large barn full of cattle and horses, and the loft full of hay for them. A snug home for ourselves and plenty to eat and drink. We raised the flax and wool from which our clothes were made. When we killed an ox or a calf, the hide was tanned to make into shoes.

But we had very little ready money. Whatever dealings we had with our neighbors was done by exchanging goods,—trading we called it. Trading was going on all the time.

One morning, as we boys were walking up the road, and had reached the upper end of Captain Esterbrook's land, Edmund said,

"Hello, Ben, look over there. Captain Joe Esterbrook and Matthew Mead are trading. Whenever you see one man sitting on a log and another walking up and down with a straw in his mouth, then they're trading. And the man with the straw in his mouth is the one anxious to have the trade go through. See how nervous Matthew is, and Captain Joe, sitting on the log whittling, looks just as calm and contented as a frog in a puddle. When you trade, Ben, don't chew a straw, but sit down and whittle. Captain Joe probably wants the trade to go through as much as Matthew does. But the whittling keeps his hands and eyes busy, and steadies his nerves. It gives him a chance to look as if he didn't care a snap about it."

Trading

"I don't think there's any need of Captain Joe whittling," said I. "He's as keen as a razor at a trade. I was going by his place a little while ago, and he had his old horse Bjax out in front of the stable, showing him to a fur trader from the Back Country, whose horse had gone lame.

"'Yes,' says he, 'he's a fine horse, kind and sound, and I wouldn't part with him for anything, if the other one hadn't died. I had a horse called Ajax, that I got off one of the professors down to the college, and the next one I bought I called Bjax. But now that Ajax is gone, there don't seem to be no sense to the name. When I had Ajax, Bjax was all right; but Bjax alone sounds sort of ridiculous, and I'll let you have him cheap.'

"His black boy, Prince, was hanging round, looking as if a funeral was going on. He stepped up, and said, 'Oh, massa, massa. Don't sell that horse. That's just the best horse we ever had.' Then the black rascal went behind the man, winked at me and grinned."

Late in the fall, after we had killed off some of the cattle, father would load a couple of pack-horses with beef and pork, which he sold in Salem. For in those days Salem was more easily reached than Boston. Probably not more than one or two families in the town spent over twenty Spanish dollars in the course of the year.

Money came most readily to those who had a handicraft, and there was hardly a house on the main road in which there was not an artificer of some kind.

Ben Apprenticed to a Blacksmith

A prudent father took care that his son learned a trade. Edmund was sent to Concord and became a cordwainer (*a worker in cordovan leather*) or shoemaker. Davy Fiske was a weaver, and soon after the fox hunt I was apprenticed to Robert Harrington, to learn the blacksmith's trade. He was a large, strong man, of a kindly nature, and was an excellent bass singer. As we worked together in his shop, with his son Thaddeus, we frequently sang psalm tunes, and his younger son Dan piped in a treble.

One day Major Ben Reed rode up, and brought his horse in to be shod.

"Well, Robert, we're going to have war again with the French. Governor Shirley's got word that they are making a settlement and building a fort down on our eastern frontier, and has ordered Colonel John Winslow to raise a regiment, and go down there to put a stop to it. Captain Frye of Littleton is raising a company, and if any of the boys want to join the expedition, they'd better enlist with him."

Davy Fiske's two older brothers, Jonathan and John, did enlist. They joined this company, and so did Joe Locke.

The regiment went up the Kennebec, built a fort, and then half of them went further up the river, to the Great Carrying Place, but found no settlements, no French nor Indians, nothing but immense and terrible swarms of black flies, midges, and bloodsucking mosquitoes; and after considerable blood was shed on both sides, they retreated and returned home.

This was but the beginning of the great struggle that we had with the French for seven long years. In the next year, 1755, early in the spring, Colonel Winslow was again ordered to beat his drums through our Province, and raise a regiment to proceed against Acadia; and Captain Spikeman began to enlist a company in our county.

The captain made his headquarters in Concord at Rowe's Tavern, which was kept by Edmund's uncle, Captain Thomas Munroe.

Several times, a sergeant, corporal, and a couple of drummers came down to Lexington, and marched through the town, beating a rub-a-dub on their drums. The sergeant would speak to the crowd, and try to get them to enlist. He would promise them—well, what wouldn't he promise them? Lands, booty, rich farms, the chance of becoming a general at least. He was an oily-tongued fellow, and Uriah Hall's son Uriah, Phineas Parker, and Tom Blanchard enlisted with him. He and his drummers stopped at our shop one day, and he came in. He placed his halberd in a corner, brushed the dust from the top of a box, and sat down.

Expedition to Acadia

"Well, which of you young men is going to serve the King? There never was such a chance for a soldier as this. Here we are, going down to the richest country in the world, to turn these

Acadians out of house and home; and any soldier who wants a farm can have it for the asking. Richest soil in the world. You can raise anything there. Level as a table, all cleared, not a stone in it, farm tools, houses and outhouses, and everything all ready for you. Hundreds of acres for the asking, and lots of booty besides. What better chance do you want?"

Mr. Harrington, who was leaning on his hammer by the forge, asked:—

"But why do you turn them out? Why don't you let them alone?"

"Why do we turn them out? Because we must. That country has belonged to England for forty-two years. And not one of those people will take the oath of allegiance. They have the easiest time in the world. Not a penny of taxes was ever asked them, and they have been treated like pet lambs. Their priests tell them not to take the oath of allegiance, and they expect every year that the King of France will retake the country."

"Well, what of it? They say they are neutrals, and if you leave them alone, and they mind their own business, and till their farms, they'll come round all right in the end."

"Will they? They're the funniest neutrals you ever saw. They are dead set against England, and claim to belong to France. If a garrison wants to buy food, not a bit will they sell. But when the French and Indians make an inroad into the country, they run to them, give them all they have, join in with them, and fight us. When the French are driven back, they scatter and go back to their farms, as innocent as can be. No, sir. There's no getting on with them. It has been tried over forty years. The only way to stop this constant trouble and fighting is to carry the whole of them out of the country, and give their rich farms to good, honest young men like these here.

The Acadians Must Be Driven Out

"Come now! Take the King's shilling. Serve his Majesty, good King George, for a few months; and you can live like lords for the rest of your days."

Thaddeus and I were mightily tempted by the man's talk, but Mr. Harrington said that he could not spare us, and that we were too young, anyhow. "And very likely, boys, instead of hundreds of acres, with houses and outhouses, and farm tools, and booty, all that you'd get would be six feet of ground and a pine box."

The days when the court sat at Concord were holidays with us, and the people flocked up there to see the court come in, and to watch the trials. And this spring, Spikeman's company was there too.

On the second day of court I rode to Concord, found Edmund at the tavern, and we went round the town together.

The court had disposed of some cases already. We saw a couple seated on the gallows, with ropes round their necks.

"Are they going to hang them, Edmund?"

"Not unless they tumble off and hang themselves. I suppose they put them up there to show that hanging would be none too good for them. Look at those fellows in the stocks. They don't belong here, and did not leave when warned out of town by the constable."

Nearby the stocks was the pillory. There was a man standing in it, with his head and hands sticking out through the holes. Of all humiliating punishments, this always seemed to me to be the worst. A man in that position looks thoroughly mean and contemptible. He appears to be put there on purpose to have something thrown at him; and it offers a temptation that boys cannot withstand.

The Pillory

"Bill Wheeler's been missing his hens right along. He suspected this man, and caught him one night, and the judge sentenced him to stand in the pillory. There's Bill over there; listen to him!"

"Well, you miserable thief, how do you like it now? I had a good deal of trouble to catch you; but it was worthwhile. You like hens? I wonder how you will like hen-fruit."

He turned aside, and I heard him say to a boy: "Here's a shilling, Hiram. They tell me eggs are pretty cheap up at the store, specially poor ones."

The boys asked the man in the pillory all manner of impudent questions. He resented it, and threatened them, when plump went a couple of eggs against the boards near his head, and the yolks spattered over his face.

"Don't! Don't you do that, boys! That's mighty mean. When I get out, won't I give you a licking!"

More eggs were thrown, and as he ducked his head, one struck him on the top of his pate. When he raised it, the yellow yolk ran down over his cheeks. Edmund and I told the boys to stop throwing eggs.

"We ain't doing nothing, and tain't your business, anyhow."

We stood guard over the boys until we saw the crowd turn toward the whipping-post; and the boys went there to see a man tied to it, and soundly thrashed on his bare back with the cat-o'-nine-tails.

"I've had enough of this, Edmund. Come over to the tavern."

The drummers were beating their drums in front of the inn, and the sergeants were telling their story of the glory, honor, and booty to be gained.

Captain Spikeman stood nearby, and if he saw a likely looking man, who seemed to be tempted, he would begin talking to him, and ask him into the tavern to have a mug of flip. Soon after, the sergeant would be called in to pin a cockade on his hat and give him the King's shilling to enlist him.

Edmund knew all the officers, who lived at the tavern, and was full of enthusiasm. "Ben, I'd like to go ever so much. I've set my heart on being a soldier. But my time isn't up, and I must serve out my apprenticeship."

Recruiting

"That's just my fix. But if the war lasts, we may get a chance yet."

In the afternoon I bade him Goodbye, and rode back home.

Chapter V: Pigeon Tuesday and its Exploits

Davy Fiske had become a weaver, as I said, and as there were several David Fiskes in town, he was called Weaver David. We used to send yarn up to him to weave, and I wore clothes made of cloth that came from his loom. Early that same spring he came down to the blacksmith's shop with one of his father's horses to be shod, and as I was getting ready, said, "Ben, it's awful to see the boys going off to the war, having all this fun fighting the French and Indians, and to be shut up in that confounded loom, listening to its clatter, when there's so much going on. Jonathan and John have just gone off again, and I must stay at home. But the pigeons are flying now, and next Tuesday will be Pigeon Tuesday. They always fly on that day. And there will be rafts of them flying down to the shore. I suppose they go to get a taste of salt, and must have it, just like the cattle. Amos Locke and I are going after them up on Bull Meadow Hill, and we want you to come too."

Wild Pigeons

"I'll go, Davy, if I can get off."

After I had shod the horse, I spoke to Mr. Harrington about it. He said, "You won't need but half a day, Ben. The shooting will be all over by nine o'clock, and you can come back and work in the afternoon."

In the spring, flights of pigeons came north very early. They lived in the woods and swamps, and as soon as it began to be light flew down to the shore.

As they came along, we used to toll them down with our decoys. The flight was almost always over by nine o'clock.

When they returned in the evening, they paid no attention to decoys, but made straight for their roost.

Tuesday morning, I was at Davy's house a couple of hours before sunrise and, as usual, found him grumbling because I had not come an hour earlier.

There was a bright moon, and we had plenty of light as we walked over the fields, and Davy told me wonderful stories of his hunting. He was full of superstitions, and had settled on this day as the one particular day in the year when there would be a great flight of pigeons.

"Pigeon Hill, off there to our right, is a pretty good place for pigeons. It's on our land, and I've got a pigeon rig up there. But Bull Meadow Hill is higher and a good deal better. It belongs to Amos's folks. He has a pigeon rig and pole on it, and it will be all ready. Amos says Bull Meadow got its name because a bull was drowned in a ditch there nigh on to a hundred years ago."

We reached Bull Meadow and went up the hill. Amos was there waiting for us.

"Where have you fellows b-been? I've been at work here for an hour and have got things pretty near ready. I put some new boughs on the booth so that it l-looks all r-right, and I've got a couple of flyers and a flutterer in that basket."

We entered the booth from the rear. The front was open from the covering to within three feet of the ground, so that we could stand up and shoot, and when we crouched down, would be hidden.

The Pigeon Rig

In front of the booth was a post about four feet high, in one side of which the end of a pole about five feet long was fastened so that it worked as if on a hinge. A string was tied to the pole and ran over the top of the post. By pulling the string, the further end of the pole could be raised or lowered by a person in the booth. Further from the booth the top and branches of a small tree had been cut off, leaving a standard twelve feet high, and to this a pole about twenty feet long had been fastened, so that it looked a good deal like a well sweep.

The end of the pole pointed toward the hut, but not directly. It slanted a little to one side in order that when the pigeons lighted on the pole we could get a good raking shot at them. Our pigeons had soft pads of leather called boots sewed round each leg to protect them from the strings which we fastened to them. We tied the strings to the boots of a pigeon, sewed a bandage over his eyes, and tied him to the further end of the pigeon stool. This was the stool pigeon. We also called him the flutterer or hoverer.

"Now give us the flyers."

Amos took out two more pigeons, and we tied long and strong strings to their boots.

"Now they're ready. But there's hardly enough string for the long flyer. We ought to let him go up at least forty feet."

"Cut a little off the string of the short flyer then, and tie it on to the other. The strings were the same length."

We looked round, to see if any pigeons were flying, but none were in sight.

"There don't seem to be any about. I'm afraid, Davy, Pigeon Tuesday won't be a success this time."

"You wait. They'll be here by and by."

"They're f-flying well now. I was f-fishing in Swithin Reed's mill p-pond, yesterday afternoon, and Venus Roe came over and said that Swithin shot a lot of pigeons in the m-morning."

A Flight in Sight

"Venus Roe! Who's she?"

"D-don't you know? She's a little black girl about twelve years old, and belongs to Swithin. Someone in B-Boston gave her to him when she was a baby."

"Oh, yes! I remember now. I've heard father tell of meeting Swithin riding out from Boston, with a keg of rum in one saddle bag, and out of the other was sticking the head of a three-year-old child."

"Here comes a flight. Send up your long flyer, Amos."

Amos threw the flyer up. We watched the pigeons. They seemed to be coming toward us.

"Now send up the short flyers."

"They're coming to us. Pull the flyers down and keep hidden. Pull away at the string, Ben, and work the pole, so that the hoverer will keep his wings fluttering. Keep on, Ben. They see him."

The pigeons flew toward the flutterer, made a swirl in the air, and began to light on the pigeon pole. We took up our guns, and as they were hovering about the pole, trying to get a foothold, we fired, and ran out and picked up twenty-nine pigeons.

"That isn't bad," said Davy. "I tell you, Pigeon Tuesday is the day. There will be more along soon."

The sky was all crimson and gold in the east. We looked toward Mt. Gilboa; the red face of the sun began to show itself. As it rose above the hill, we heard the stroke of the bell.

"Some one's d-dead.—Hark! Only one stroke. It's a child. One for a c-child, two for a woman, and three strokes for a man."

"I know who it is. Father was called up to Sam Hadley's last night. Little Benoni Mead was very poorly, and they didn't think he'd last through the night."

Poor little Benoni! His father, Cornelius Mead, had died of camp fever in the war; his mother and he had come on the town for support, and had been boarded with her brother, Sam Hadley, not far from Bull Meadow Hill. Benoni had always been ailing, and of late had failed rapidly.

Another Flight of Pigeons

"Well, boys," said Davy, "let's get back to work. It won't do Benoni any good to be mooning round."

We watched for pigeons again, and another small flight came along. We worked our decoys and got twenty.

After that we waited a long time,—until nearly nine o'clock. Then Davy and I gave it up, and decided to go home. Davy had some work to do. But Amos said he would stay a little while longer. We made a division of our pigeons, and Davy and I started for home.

We had not gone more than half a mile when we saw a terrible big flight.

"I wonder if Amos will get a shot at them, Ben. Let's get back as quick as we can. We may be in time."

We threw down our pigeons, and made through the woods as fast as we could. As we were running up the hill, we heard a bang.

"Confound the luck," said Davy, "we're just too late! Let's hurry up and help Amos."

When we got to the top of the hill Amos was running round, twisting the necks of the wounded pigeons. As soon as he saw us, he stood up and began:—

"H-H-He—" But he was too excited, and couldn't get the words out. He pointed to the pigeons, and kept on catching them and twisting their necks. We did the same. When we got through,

Davy asked, "What was it that you were saying to us when we got here? I didn't quite catch it."

"No! It sort er st-stuck on the way; 'h-help me' is pretty hard to say sometimes. I t-t-tell you, b-boys, there was millions of 'em, an-and I guess I shot a barrel full. When I saw that b-big flight coming, I wished you were here, and then I was g-glad you were not. For I w-wanted to see h-how many I should get. They came just like a b-big cloud, and began to light on that p-pole, and the air was just f-full of them. You c-couldn't see anything but pigeons. I blazed away, and the ground was c-covered with them.

"I was t-tickled enough to see you fellows jump in and help me. I w-wonder how many there are. Let's count them."

Amos Makes a Great Shot

We gathered them up, and there were fifty-two.

"Hurrah! One f-for every week in the year!"

Amos had a good many adventures in his life afterward, fighting with the French and Indians. But that shot was the one particular thing that made life a joy to him.

Chapter VI: A Pauper's Funeral—Ben's Friend the Minister, and Ben's Victory in Wrestling

When I returned to the shop, Mr. Harrington said, "I'm glad you're back, Ben. The rest of the selectmen have left the care of Benoni Mead's funeral to me, and I've got a lot of things to do. We must have some gloves and scarves for the bearers, and you'll have to ride down to Charlestown to buy them."

I mounted a horse and rode through Menotomy and over the Plains. There was a sharp breeze blowing; and as I neared the Neck, I heard a creaking as if a rusty hinge was being turned.

Looking to the left, I saw a negro hanging in gallows at the foot of a ledge. The wind made the body sway to and fro, and the grating of the chains caused the noise. The sight made cold shivers go up my back, and I hurried on until I reached Cheever's store near the Boston ferry and bought the gloves and scarves.

Benoni's Funeral

On the next day little Benoni was buried. Days on which there were funerals were half-holidays that everyone might attend. When I arrived at the Hadley house, there were a number of men near the door, and others leaning on the fence. The town bier stood in front of the house, and the pall was over it.

I went into the house and looked at Benoni. His thin little face was peaceful and happy as if he had found rest and an end of pain. Old Seth Green slouched in after me. Winter pig we used to call him, he was so sleek and fat. He looked at Benoni with a woebegone expression, and, turning away, helped himself to some liquor which stood on a table.

I followed him out and heard him say to Amos Muzzy: "Have you been in to see Benoni? Looks real sweet and pretty. Mighty good rum the town provided. Some of Buckman's best. Poor little fellow! I think I'll go in and take another look at him."

The minister, Mr. Clark, now came. He made a short prayer, and then the coffin was placed on the bier and covered with the pall. Some of the most prominent men in the town were the pall-bearers. They placed the bier on their shoulders, and the procession followed them. As we passed the meeting house, the bell tolled. When we reached the burying yard, the coffin was lowered into the grave. The minister made another short prayer. Earth was thrown on the coffin, the grave was filled in, and we departed.

I say the minister, Mr. Clark. For some time after the death of Mr. Hancock we had no settled pastor. Ministers came and preached awhile for us and then departed. We had become so accustomed to the old bishop that it seemed as if no one could satisfy us or fill his place. It was not until late in the previous year that we found the man who suited.

Mr. Jonas Clark, a young college graduate, preached to us, and we were mutually pleased. The town voted to request him to become our pastor. He accepted, and was ordained in November. The town voted one hundred pounds for the celebration. The Governor's Council came out from Boston. Deputations were sent from the surrounding towns, and we had a great time, hours of preaching and hours of feasting. People loved Mr. Hancock for his great common sense, his bluff, hearty, jovial manner, and the wit and humor that abounded in him at a time when most ministers thought it their duty to look as solemn as a gravestone.

The New Minister

Mr. Clark became as much beloved and respected as Mr. Hancock, and yet he did not resemble him. His manners were elegant. He was learned, able, and very polite. Neat as wax, he made us feel ashamed of our slovenly ways. He was not the bluff, hale fellow the old bishop was, who compelled us to do what he knew was right.

Mr. Clark had a kind heart, a keen, clear mind. Though he guided us with a firm hand, it was done in such a gentle and polite manner, that we rarely felt how completely we were under his control.

And though he was a student and his tastes were delicate, still he did not frown upon our rude sports, provided they were not low or brutal. "They make the body erect and supple and give strength and elasticity to the muscles. The body should be cultivated as well as the mind. What we want is a sound mind in a sound body."

Wrestling was the great sport in those days, and I was always fond of it. I was very strong naturally, and my trade as blacksmith had toughened my muscles wonderfully.

Our strongest man and best wrestler was Jonas Parker. You would hardly have suspected it; for though he had rather a grim, determined look, he was a quiet, staid, religious man and a great lover of reading.

A few years before, he had bought some land of Dr. Fiske and built a house not far from Bishop Hancock's and constantly borrowed and read his books.

He was also a great lover of wrestling, knew all the tricks, and had the reputation of being the best man in our county at it.

Ben Practices Wrestling

He watched me wrestling with the other boys, and one day said to me: "Ben, you've got the making of a great wrestler in you. Come up to my house when you can, and I'll teach you what I know about it."

On holidays and whenever I got a chance, I went up to his place, and we would walk down to a grove back of his barn and wrestle. We kept this up all the spring and summer, and he taught me the different throws.

He said, "You're coming on at a great rate, Ben. When you get your full strength, I think you'll be as good or a better wrestler than I am, and there's not such a great difference even now. I don't think we had ever better wrestle in earnest, for it might make bad blood between us. We can wrestle together for practice and leave it undecided which is the better man."

After wrestling we would go into the house, and he would take out a book of plays by William Shakespeare and read from it to me. We were both religious men and did not believe in play acting. But plays like these could do no harm. Jonas loved this man's writings next to the Bible, and I saved up money and bought a copy of the book myself. Mr. Clark had the same love for Shakespeare, and often when we stopped wrestling, as it began to grow dark, Jonas would say that Mr. Clark had asked him to come down to his house with me, and he would read to us. The plays seemed much finer as he read them in his clear voice and explained them to us, for by ourselves we only saw a portion of their beauties.

Jonas and I were at his house one August evening of this year, 1757, and Mr. Clark had just begun to read, when Dr. Fiske rode up, and pulling up his horse, called out: "Mr. Clark! Mr. Clark! There's bad news—very bad news from the army. Colonel Brattle has received word from General Webb that the French army were advancing to attack Fort William Henry, and he was afraid it would be taken. Goodbye!"

Mr. Clark shut up the book and said, "This is no night for Shakespeare. Let us pray for the safety of our army."

Bad News from the Army

Two days afterward, another messenger rode up to our shop.

"There has been a great disaster. Fort William Henry is taken, and the garrison has been massacred."

"Go on! How did it happen?"

"Colonel Munro was at the fort with a small force. Montcalm advanced with his army to attack it. Munro sent to Webb for reinforcements. He promised to send them and did send a few. Munro again asked for more men, but Webb didn't let a man go. Montcalm attacked the fort, battered it to pieces, and finally the garrison was compelled to surrender. They were to deliver up their arms and then were to be allowed to march off to the English army. They gave up their guns and started back to Webb, but before they got far they were set upon by the Indians and most of them massacred. Some few escaped to Webb's army."

"And what was Webb doing all this time?"

"Shaking in his shoes, I guess. He is now; for he has sent messengers everywhere for reinforcements."

"The miserable coward! We'll send him men, but he ought to be hanged."

The next day a number of men set out under Captain Blodgett.

I wished to go very much, but Mr. Harrington said, "It's too late in the season for them to do anything. They will just sit down and watch each other. Your time is up next spring, and if you want to go then, I'll let you off early."

So I stayed at home, and it was well I did, for the company only got as far as Springfield, where they were met by messengers from Webb, who had got over his fright, telling them to return. They came back to Lexington, having been out only twelve days.

When they returned, we had a great jollification. The company marched to the training field, and went through the exercises. Crowds gathered round and ate gingerbread and drank beer.

A lot of worthless fellows used to wander round the country, and pick up a living by wrestling and betting on themselves. Such a man appeared on the training field that day.

The Essex County Champion

"Here I am, boys, at your service,—Sam Sloan, the champion wrestler of Essex County. I've wrestled with the best men of every town in the county,—Newburyport, Ipswich, Gloucester, Marblehead, Salem,—and thrown them all. I've been from one end of the county to the other, and not a man can stand up against me. I hear you've got the best man in Middlesex in this town, and I've come to throw him. If you think I can't, make your bets. I've got ten pounds with me, and I want to bet every penny of it."

He found plenty of men who were ready to bet with him, for all had confidence in Jonas.

Someone ran after Jonas and brought him to the place where this man was boasting.

"So, you're Jonas Parker, the best man in Middlesex? Well, you look as if you could wrestle a bit, but you'll know more about it, after I get through with you."

Jonas said nothing, but took off his jacket and waistcoat, and looked at him quietly, with a grim smile.

Then they grappled each other, and I watched them anxiously. It did not seem to me that Jonas was exerting himself fully or doing his very best. But the man from Essex was laid on the ground in a short time.

He jumped up furious. "That was an accident. Just a piece of bad luck. My foot slipped on something in the grass. It wasn't a fair wrestle. Come on and try it again. I can throw you as easy as tumbling off a log."

"Wait a minute," said Jonas; "pay your bets, and then we'll talk."

The man pulled out his wallet, paid his bets, and said, "Now, come on, and I'll show you what wrestling is."

"Wait a bit," said Jonas; "don't hurry! You talk big. But you must first prove that you are a wrestler. There's a likely lad here, and if you wrestle him, and show that you can wrestle, you can take an hour's time to get fresh, and I'll try you again."

The man blustered; but Jonas turned away, and coming to me, said, "Now, Ben, I want you to show these people what there is in you. You can throw him if you only make up your mind to it. You are very strong in the arms, and if I were you, I'd give him a grip at first just to show him your strength, and to put a little fear into him."

A Likely Lad

Father stepped up, and said, "Jonas, what are you up to? Ben can never wrestle that man."

"Neighbor Comee! You don't know what Ben can do at wrestling, and I do. And faith! I have a suspicion he's the best wrestler in the county."

Then Jonas led me to the man. "This is the lad."

"Lad! Why, he's as big as you be. How old are you?"

"Twenty, sir."

"Well, come on."

We caught hold of each other, and I gave him a grip that made him gasp. We broke away, and he looked at me, panting, and said,

"What be ye, anyhow? You've got a hug like a black bear."

"Oh, that's nothing. That's just a little love squeeze to show you how much I like you."

"Well, come on again; I'll show you what wrestling is."

He was not so strong as I, and I hustled him round in a lively way; but he knew a good deal about wrestling, and kept his feet well. We struggled for a while, and I squeezed him and shook him up, and then tried Jonas's pet throw. He went to the ground like a log, and lay there stunned.

I was scared at first, for I thought I had killed him, but Jonas said, "He's all right, Ben. Just stand back, boys, and give him a little air."

He came to in a short time, sat up, and after looking about him got up and said, "A likely lad! I should say so. A kind of mixture of bear, wildcat, and greased lightning. I must get out of this town quick, or you'll be setting some child at me, and I don't know what would happen."

He jammed his hat on his head, took his coat and waistcoat under his arm, and hurried away.

Of course, I got great credit and praise, for no one but Jonas knew that I was a first-class wrestler; and the men all felt proud to have another man in the town almost as good at it as Jonas.

Ben Warned Against False Pride

Amos and Davy had been staring at me, open-mouthed. Both of them came up and shook hands with me in a most respectful manner. Father took me by the arm and walked home with me, giving me a lecture all the way on the vanity of foolish games and warning me to beware of a false pride in my strength.

But when I had taken the basin, and was washing my face and hands by the back door, I could hear him telling mother about it, as jubilant as one of those old Hebrews over the fall of his enemies.

Goodness! If I had displayed the vanity and false pride that he showed over me, I don't know what punishment he would not have given me.

When I came in, he bottled himself up, and looked at me in a sad, reproving manner. But I knew he was as happy as a man could be. Mother did not like it, and I had to assure her again and again that I was not hurt. She began to talk about giving me some herb tea, and I got out of the house as quickly as possible.

Chapter VII: Tales From the Frontier—Mr. Tithingman and His Services

This long war was a terrible strain on our Province. Some man from almost every family in town was with the army at Lake George. The value of our currency had fallen, and nearly one-half of what we earned and produced went to pay the heavy taxes.

The Provinces did not work well together. There were rivalries and dissensions among them. The French were united, and their army was led by an able commander, the Marquis Montcalm.

Our generals were mostly incompetent men who owed their positions to influence at court.

We kept up the bitter struggle, hoping that at last we should have a general capable of coping with Montcalm.

Edmund Enlists

It was a gloomy time, but we kept pegging away in a resolute manner, for it was a question whether we or the French should be masters of this country; whether we should keep our farms and have a roof over our heads or should be overrun by murderous Indians. And arrangements were made to have a larger army in the field than ever before.

About the middle of January, Edmund sent me word from Concord that Captain Robert Rogers was enlisting men for a new company in his corps of Rangers. He said, "I have joined the company and have been made sergeant. Rogers will return to Boston by the way of Lexington and will stay overnight at Jonathan Raymond's tavern. Come up there sure and see me."

As father and I were working in the barn, I said to him: "Father, I think the time has come when I ought to go to the war. You promised that I might enlist in the spring. But I'd a good deal rather go with this man Rogers and do some fighting than sit round doing nothing and die of camp disease as the rest of the army have been doing."

He kept on for a while pitching the hay down in front of the cattle, and then leaned on his pitchfork.

"Well, Ben, I suppose you really ought to go. One man out of every four in the Province is in the army, and we should do our share. I am too old. John has just got married, and David is but a boy. You're the right age and the one to go. I think as you do, that it's better to do some fighting, and take one's chances of being killed by a bullet rather than by camp fever.

"Those French and Indians killed and scalped my brother John, and since this war began I have often wanted to have a hand in it myself, to get even with them, but I'm too old.

"You can go, Ben. There's lots of miserable wretches and immorality and profanity among the regulars. I want you to remain a good boy, as you always have been. I need not tell you to be brave. You will be that.

"Ben, I scolded you about that wrestling match, but I was awful proud of you and happy over it."

The Raymond Tavern

"I knew that, father. Do you suppose I didn't notice you chuckling to yourself when you thought no one saw you?"

"Well, I suppose you did, you young rascal; I couldn't help it, I was that surprised and delighted. To think of Jonas Parker telling me he didn't know but that you were a better wrestler than he. And to see you hustle that man about and throw him made me so proud that I felt ashamed and humbled. And when you thought I was scolding you, I was really reproving my own sinful vanity and pride."

After supper we went up to the Raymond Tavern. Quite a crowd of men were in the barroom. They were seated in front of a great fire of logs and peat. Captain Rogers was in their midst.

Edmund came up, and made us acquainted with the captain. He shook hands with me, and turning to father, said,—

"This is a likely young fellow, Mr. Comee. I wish I could have him with me in my corps."

"It is possible," said father. "We have had some slight talk about it. We will think it over."

Rogers was a big man, over six feet high, well proportioned, and apparently very strong. Later on I learned that his strength was wonderful. His features were prominent, strong, but not agreeable. His eyes were not good eyes. At times, a hard, cruel look came into his face.

He seemed to be a man of great hardihood, of great presence of mind, keen and unscrupulous,—a man I should not wish for a neighbor.

In answer to a remark that he must find his present life quite different from his former life, as a farmer, he said,—

"Not a bit! I never was a farmer. I was brought up in the woods on the frontier among wild animals and Indians. My father was a hunter and trapper. One day he went out hunting and toward night started to visit another hunter at his hut in the woods. His friend mistook him in the twilight and shot him. All my life has been spent in the woods, either hunting or trading with the French and Indians, or else fighting them."

A Bowl of Flip

Hepzibah Raymond came in with a bowl of flip—the proper mixture of rum, malt beer, and brown sugar.

She set it down on the hearth, and her son John, a cripple, who was seated in the fireplace, drew one of the iron loggerheads out of the fire, where half a dozen of them were always being heated. He hit it against the andiron to knock the ashes off, and plunged it into the mixture. A pleasant smell arose from it; he waited until it foamed up, and then drew the loggerhead out. Hepzibah passed the bowl to Captain Rogers.

"Here's to good King George and confusion to his enemies!"

He took a long draught at it, and then the bowl was passed round.

A man of middle age came into the room, with a whip in his hand, and his hat jammed well on his head.

"Good evening, Ephraim."

"Sarvent, (*distinguished*) sirs!"

"Captain, this is Ephraim Winship. He knows something about Indian fighting. Show him your head, Ephraim."

Ephraim took off his hat, and lifted his wig from his head. He had but one eye. There were two bare red spots on top of his head, and between them a fringe of hair ran back from his forehead. It gave him a weird appearance.

"Hello!" said Rogers. "You've been among the Indians, haven't you? How did you lose your scalp or scalps? For I see you have lost two."

The men made room for Ephraim. He put on his wig and sat down.

"I have to keep those spots pretty well covered up these winter nights, or I have all sorts of trouble with my head.

"I had been living down on the Eastern Frontier for some years at a place called New Marblehead. We had plenty of scares, but no real trouble with the Indians, until this war broke out. It was in May, two years ago. I went out with Ezra Brown, to do some work on his farm, which was a mile from the garrison house where we lived. We had a guard of four men and four lads. Ezra and I were ahead. As we were walking through some woods, the Indians—there were fifteen to twenty of them—fired at us. I felt a twinge in my shoulder and a terrible pain in my eye. Then came a thump on my head. When I came to, I was in bed at the garrison house, with my scalp, or rather scalps, gone, for I have two bumps on top of my head, and they took a scalp from each bump. My right eye was gone, and I had a bullet in the shoulder.

Ephraim's Adventure

"Poor Ezra was killed at the first volley and scalped. An Indian hit me on the head with his tomahawk; but I have a good thick skull, and the blow glanced, and only stunned me.

"Some of our men ran to the fort, but my boy Gershom rallied the rest, and they fought the Indians, who were double their number. Both parties got behind trees, and tried to pick each other off.

"Old Poland, their chief, fired, and in reloading exposed himself, and was shot. Then the Indians gave an infernal screech and ran over to him.

"As they did so, our men shot two more of them, and they picked up their dead and carried them off."

"You had a narrow squeak of it, that time," said Rogers. "I never was scalped, but I've been near it times enough."

Hepzibah brought in more bowls of flip, and we watched John plunge the red-hot loggerheads in, until the foam arose, and the bitter-sweet smell filled the room.

We were passing the bowls round, and drinking the flip, when Matthew Mead, the tithingman, came in. He sat down and watched us. Then he went over to John Perry, and said, "Don't drink any more, John. You have had enough."

John let the bowl go by, for if he had disobeyed the warning of the tithingman, he would have been punished by the magistrate, or would have been reprimanded publicly in meeting.

"Oh, come now, Mr. Tithingman," said Rogers. "Don't spoil the sport. A little flip does no one any harm. Sit down and join us."

The Tithingman

"There's no doubt," said Matthew, as they passed him the bowl, and he took a long swig at it, "that flip is a good drink. I like it, and so does neighbor John Perry. But it must be allowed that it's a most insinuating drink, sweet and treacherous. And neighbor John has had enough. But the rest of the company can drink a little longer. We have heard great stories of your adventures, captain, and would like to have you tell us some of them."

Then Rogers told us tales of hair-breadth escapes, and of encounters with the enemy, that made our hearts beat quick, as we listened to him. Of scouts through the woods, in which they inspect the enemy's forts and make plans of them. How they crept up close to the fort and captured a vedette (*guard*) within two gun-shots of the gate. How they hauled whaleboats over a mountain, embarked at the lower end of Lake Champlain, rowed down the lake at night, and after hiding in the daytime, attacked the enemy's boats, and sunk them.

He told of an expedition he made the previous January, with Captain Spikeman, Lieutenant John Stark and seventy-four men.

"We went down Lake George on skates, and then through the woods back of Fort Ticonderoga on snowshoes. When we got to Lake Champlain, we lay in wait for the enemy's sleds, which were coming up the lake loaded with provisions. We captured three sleds and seven prisoners, but some of the French escaped. We learned that the fort had been reinforced, and knew that they would have notice of our presence. Our guns were wet, for it had been raining, and we went back to our fires and dried them. Then we marched hastily toward Fort William Henry. About noon we were waylaid by a large party of the enemy. We fought all the afternoon, until nightfall, when we separated and escaped through the woods to Lake George. I received two wounds in the fight. I sent messengers to the fort for help, for many could go no further. Forty-eight of us out of seventy-four got back with our prisoners. You may think, friends, that this was a bad defeat, but we learned afterward that we fought against two hundred and fifty men, and killed one hundred and sixteen of them. Your old friend Captain Spikeman was killed in the fight."

A Successful Defeat

The bowls of flip had been going round while Rogers was talking, and finally Matthew Mead said,—

"Well, neighbors, I think we are getting toward the state where neighbor John was when I came, and we'd better all go home."

As we rose, Rogers said, "I want some of you fellows with me this coming campaign, and we'll make things lively for the French up around Fort Ti and have some fun. I count on you, Comee."

Chapter VIII: Ben and Amos Join Rogers's Rangers and March to the West

A few days after this, Amos and I went up to Concord and enlisted in the Rangers. We had no showy uniform. Our clothes were of strong homespun of a dull color that would not attract attention in the woods. We brought our own guns, and they gave each of us a blanket, a greatcoat, a hatchet, and a wooden bottle in which to carry our drink. We were also given rackets and skates.

We waited until the end of January, when Rogers marched into town with five companies of men whom he had collected in New Hampshire. Most of them were rough, stern frontiersmen from the Amoskeag Falls, skilled in Indian fighting.

The recruits from Middlesex were distributed among these companies, and Edmund had us placed in his squad. On my right in the ranks was McKinstry, a grizzled old trapper, and to the left was John Martin, a hardy fellow a few years older than myself. Both of them had served before with Rogers.

Rogers Instructs the Rangers

Four of the companies set sail from Boston for Cape Breton, to take part in the siege of that place, and our company, under Rogers, started on the march for Fort Edward. The snow was deep, and we travelled on snowshoes. Rogers made us march in single file, with a man some distance ahead, and another behind. On either side were flankers to detect the enemy. As we shuffled along over the snow he taught us how to act in a hostile country.

"Don't crowd up together. Keep several paces apart. Then if the enemy fires at you, one shot will not hit two men. When you come to low, marshy ground, change the order of your march and go abreast, for if you went in single file, you would wear a path in the ground that the enemy could follow. If you are to reconnoiter a place, make a stand in a safe spot when you get near it, and send a couple of men ahead to look the ground over. If you have to retreat and come to a river, cross it anywhere but at the usual ford, for that is where the enemy would hide on the farther side ready to pick you off. If your march is by a lake or river, keep at some distance from it, that you may not be hemmed in on one side and caught in a trap. When you go out, always return by a different way, and avoid the usual travelled paths."

Thus, as we marched along, Rogers kept talking to us, instructing us in the methods of wood-fighting.

We went through Worcester, Brookfield, and Northampton to Pontoosuc Fort, where a party of Mohegan Indians from Stockbridge joined us, under their chief Jacob. Then to a Dutch settlement called Kinderhook, and to the Hudson River. The weather was very cold, and the river was frozen over. Rogers told us to put on our skates, and we skated up the river to Fort Edward.

This was a very strong fort, with much artillery. The fort was on the left shore, and a very strong blockhouse was on the right bank. The Rangers' camp was on an island in the Hudson. Their barracks were made of logs, with bark roofs, and their camp was not in bad condition.

Hatred Of Indians

The Rangers were mostly frontiersmen from New Hampshire, who had lived in the woods all their lives, and had fought against wild beasts and Indians. The life they were now leading was simply their old life on a larger scale. Most of them were dressed in deerskin. They were rough, stern men, who had been so much exposed to danger, and were so used to it, that they seemed to have no fear. They looked upon the French and Indians as a dire plague, to be wiped off the earth by any means. They had heard the war-whoop at their own homes, and had seen their close relatives scalped by Indians. No wonder they classed the redskins with wolves and snakes, as a plague to be wiped off the earth. Living in the woods so much, they seemed to have acquired the keen senses that wild animals have. They were ever on the alert. Their eyes and ears noticed all the signs and sounds of nature. They had fought savages for years, and their own ways were savage. Many of them took scalps.

I do not believe that a bolder or more adventurous set of men than these Rangers ever existed.

As I looked them over and saw what a lot of keen, fearless, and self-reliant men I was among, I was very proud to think that I was one of this chosen corps.

McKinstry said, "They're a tough set, Ben. But when you get in your first fight, you'll be glad you're with a tough set. Not much school learning among them; but they know all about the woods and Injun fighting, and that's what we want here."

Every evening at roll-call we formed on parade, equipped with a firelock, sixty rounds of powder and ball, and a hatchet, and were inspected, that we might be ready at a minute's warning. The guards were arranged and the scouts for the next day appointed.

After we had been at the camp a couple of days Rogers came out of his hut and said to me:—

"Come, Comee, I'm going over to the fort and may want someone to bring back a few things."

The Black Watch

We crossed the ice to the shore and went up to the fort. It was a great sight for me to see the regulars in their bright scarlet coats, the Scotch Highlanders with their kilts and tartans, and our own provincial troops in blue, though there were not many of them, as they had mostly gone home for the winter.

Rogers walked up to the headquarters of Colonel Haviland, the commander.

"I shall be busy here some time. Come back in an hour and wait for me."

I went over to the Scotch regiment, the Black Watch it was called, and listened to them talking their curious language.

One of the men turned to me and asked if I was looking for anyone.

"Well, I'm of Scotch descent, and I thought I'd see if there were any McComees or Munros among you."

He looked over to another group and shouted: "Hector! Hector Munro! Here's one of your kinsmen." A strong, active fellow of some twenty-eight or thirty years came over.

"How's that? I didn't know that any of our kin were over here."

"My grandmother was a Munro, and her father was taken prisoner while fighting for King Charles the First, and was sent to America."

"Hear that now! My brother Donald and myself were out with Charlie in forty-five, and we had a hard time of it afterward, hunted about until they made up their minds to form some Highland regiments and give pardon to those who enlisted, and here we are fighting for King George."

He led me to his brother and made me acquainted with him. We went to their quarters, and I learned more about the clan in a short time than I ever heard before or since. It seemed as if most of the great generals in almost every army were Munros, and they traced their ancestry back to the time of Noah.

At last I said that I must go to headquarters to meet Captain Rogers.

Rogers Assumes England's Debt

"So you belong to the Rangers? They're a braw set of men, and there's many a gude Scotchman among them. We'll come over and see you."

I returned and waited for Rogers, and when he came out, he said, "Come over to the sutler's hut; I want to buy some things we haven't got on the island."

Rogers made some purchases and then listened to two English officers who were seated at a table, drinking. They had reached a maudlin state, and were bewailing the fate of England.

"This is a sad day for old England, my boy."

"Yes, the country will never be able to stand up under the great debt that we have incurred for these miserable Provinces."

Rogers went over to them and said,—

"Don't let that trouble you, my friends. Make yourselves easy on that score, for I will pay half the national debt, and my good friend here says he will take the other half on his shoulders, and the nation will be rid of her difficulties."

"By Gad! I'm blessed if you're not fine fellows. Sit down and have a drink with us."

Rogers introduced me to them as the Earl of Middlesex. They took off their hats to me and ordered some grog for us. I barely tasted mine, for I had no heart to drink with the besotted fools. We bade them Goodbye, I took up the things which Rogers had bought, and we walked away.

"Well, Comee, we've settled the nation's debt. That's one good thing off our hands. There's another thing I wish we could get rid of as easily. The old country has sent us over some curious commanders. There was Braddock, who threw away his army and his life; Webb, who was a coward; Loudon, our present commander, is always running hither and thither, giving orders, but affecting nothing. He is like the pictures of St. George on the tavern signs,—always on horseback, but never getting anywhere. But this Colonel Haviland, the commandant here, beats them all hollow. A worse specimen of stupidity or rascality I never saw. Captain Israel Putnam of the Connecticut troops was sent out on a scout a week ago. Before he went, Haviland said publicly that on his return he should send me out against the French with four hundred men. One of Putnam's men deserted to the enemy and one of the Rangers was captured, so that the enemy knew all about it. Putnam says there are about six hundred Indians near Ticonderoga; and now this Haviland sends me out, not with four hundred men, but with one hundred and eighty, all told. You will see all the fighting you want inside the next week and I hope we may both get through it alive."

A Pleasant Prospect

When I returned to the island, I told Edmund and Amos what Rogers had said, and we felt pretty glum. "It looks to me," said Edmund, "as if the rest of the campaign wouldn't interest us very much."

THE BATTLE ON SNOW SHOES!!

Chapter IX: In Which the Rangers Engage With the French and Indians

On the 10th of March we set forth on snowshoes and travelled through the thick forest. That night we encamped at a brook. The Rangers built shelters of boughs in a short time. Big fires were made, and after we had our suppers and a pull at the pipe, we rolled ourselves up in our blankets and went to sleep.

The next morning we reached Lake George, and saw the blackened ruins of Fort William Henry, where the massacre had taken place some eight months before.

Of course I knew the story, but Martin had been there, and told me how the fort was besieged by Montcalm; and after it was battered to pieces, the garrison surrendered. They had given up their arms and were marching back to the English army, when the drunken Indians set upon them and killed and scalped most of the force. Martin caught up a little boy whose parents had been killed, and escaped through the dense woods.

An Alarm

We marched down the lake in three files, threading our way among the islands and skirting the steep cliffs. The lake stretched out before us, covered with thick ice. On the further side were the woods and mountains.

We camped near the First Narrows that night. The next day we turned away from the lake and went to a cape called Sebattis Point.

"What's the matter, Martin? Why do we halt?"

"Didn't you see a dog run across the lake, some distance down?"

"Yes, I saw something go across."

"Well, it was a dog, and if there was a dog, there were probably Indians with him. What would a dog be doing out here alone?"

We camped in the woods, and after it was dark skated down the lake.

Our advanced guard sent back word that they thought they had seen a fire on an island. We hid our hand-sleighs and packs and went there, but could find no signs of a fire.

Rogers said that very likely it was the light from some old rotten stumps, but Martin was not of this opinion.

"There was a fire there. First we see the dog, and then the fire. The fire could be put out, and it would be difficult to find the burnt sticks in the dark. If it were the light from old wood, someone of all this party would have seen it. The French are no fools. They knew we were coming, and some Indians are watching us. We'll have a hot time before we get back."

We now left the lake, lest we should be seen, and marched through the woods back of the mountain which overlooked Fort Ticonderoga. At noon we halted.

Rogers said, "We are about two miles from the advanced guard of the French. We will wait here a couple of hours, and then go on. When night comes, we will make an ambush in the paths, and capture some of the guards as they come out in the morning."

An Ambush

We started on again, with a brook on our left and a steep mountain on our right.

We kept a sharp watch on the brook, for the enemy would probably travel on it, as the snow was four feet deep.

Our advanced guard came back and reported that the enemy were ahead. That there were ninety of them, mostly Indians. They were coming down the brook. The bank of the brook was higher than the ground where we were, and Rogers gave the order:—

"Come, boys! Stretch out in a line behind the bank. Lie down and keep hidden. Wait until I give the signal by firing my gun, and then jump up and give it to them."

Rogers hid in a clump of bushes, from which he could look over the bank. We lay without stirring, until Rogers fired and shouted, "Now, boys."

We jumped up and fired at them. It was the first time I had seen Indians, and very hideous they looked, as I stood up and saw them on the brook, dressed in moccasins, leggings, and breech clout, with a mantle or cloak of skins over their shoulders, a feather in the scalp-lock, and their faces and breasts painted with stripes of red and black.

When we fired, a great number of them fell, and the rest ran away. We supposed that they were defeated, and pursued them. But we got into a hornets' nest. For this was only the advanced guard, and as we ran after them, several hundred more French and Indians came up, fired at us, and killed nearly fifty of our men. I could hear the bullets whistle by me, and men dropped at my side.

We rallied and retreated; and having reloaded, poured a volley into them that drove them back again.

"What do you think about that fire on the island, Ben?" asked Martin.

They came on a third time, in front and on both sides of us. We kept up a continual fire and drove the flanking parties back, and they retreated once more.

Warm Work

When that great body of French and Indians appeared and their fierce war-whoops sounded through the woods, when the firing began and the men fell down close by me, I must confess I was nervous and frightened. But I looked on either side, and there stood the grim, stern frontiersmen picking off their men as cool as if they were at a turkey shoot. This brought my confidence back at once, and as the fight became hot, I found myself filled with an angry rage. I wanted to kill, to kill as many as I could, and pay off the old score.

We backed up against the steep mountain. The Indians now tried to go up it on our right, but a party was sent out and repulsed them. Another party attempted to ascend on our left. They, too, were driven back. Edmund, Amos, and I were with the main body, fighting, loading, and shooting as fast as we could. No time for talk. Sometimes the Indians were twenty yards from us, and at times we were all mixed up with them, fighting hand to hand.

When I had fired, I pulled out my hatchet, and as these devilish-looking savages in their red and black paint rushed at me, I cut and hacked with my hatchet in my right hand, and holding my firelock in my left, warded off the blows with it. A blow on my arm knocked the hatchet from my hand. Then I used my gun as a club. It was a long, heavy, old firelock, and anger and excitement added to my strength, so that it was a terrible weapon. I smashed away with it until nothing was left but the bent barrel.

When we drove them back, I picked up a French gun and a hatchet. There were plenty of them, for dead and dying men lay in heaps on the ground.

We struggled with them an hour and a half, during which time we lost over one hundred men.

Rogers was in the thick of the fight most of the time. Yet he saw what was going on round us, and directed our movements. Toward dark he cried out: "It's no use, boys; we must get out of this place. Follow me."

We ran up the mountain to a spot where Lieutenant Phillips and some men were fighting a flanking party of Indians, and there we had another lively scrimmage. We went along the side of the mountain. I had lost my rackets. One couldn't think of them and fight, as we had been fighting, too.

An Encounter

Rogers shouted: "Scatter, boys! Every man for himself. Meet at the First Narrows."

I loaded my gun and floundered along in the deep snow, making all possible haste.

Looking behind, I saw that an Indian on snowshoes was following me. I started up a side hill, where his rackets would not give him an advantage.

He fired, but missed me. I turned and shot him, as he raised his hand to throw his tomahawk. He fell and was quite dead by the time I reached him.

It's no pleasant sight to look on the face of a man you have just killed, even though you have right on your side, and he be only a redskin.

One glance at that face and the staring eyes was enough. I felt weak and guilty as I knelt by him, and picked up his rackets, gun, and ammunition. I took his fur mantle, too, for I had thrown away my blanket, and knew that I should be cold before the night was over.

I wandered through the woods until the moon rose, and gave me the direction to take. Then I came to the lake and went out on it, and at last got to the Narrows, where I found what was left of our party. Edmund and Amos were with them. Rogers had sent a messenger for assistance.

Over two-thirds of our party were killed or missing. And of those who remained, there were but few who did not have some cut or bullet wound.

We were exhausted. The men had thrown away their blankets, and the night was bitter cold.

We could not have fires, as they would have been beacon lights to the enemy, showing them where we were.

We huddled together like sheep for warmth, and I gave my mantle to a poor fellow who was badly wounded.

They Return to Fort Edward

When the day began to break, we marched up the lake, and were met by Captain Stark with reinforcements, and sleds for our wounded, and then proceeded to Fort Edward.

The next day, as Edmund, Amos, and I were talking the fight over, Rogers came to us. He laughed, and said, "Well, boys! You haven't been here long. But you've had lots of fun, haven't you?"

"Yes, sir. Plenty! We are satisfied. We can stand a long spell of dull times now."

The Rangers lost so heavily in this fight that but little was required of them for some time. A few scouting-parties were sent out, but they were of little consequence.

Chapter X: Lord Howe and His Death—The Loyalty of John Stark

Early in the spring, Lord Loudon was recalled, and General Abercrombie was appointed in his stead, with young Lord Howe as second in command.

Abercrombie was the kind of English general to which we were accustomed,—a dull, heavy man, who owed his position to influence at court. We put little faith in him. But Lord Howe gained our hearts and confidence at once.

It was well understood in the army that Lord Howe was sent over to furnish the brains and ability in this campaign, and was to direct the fighting, and that General Abercrombie was to reap the benefit.

Lord Howe spent much of his time among the Rangers, and went out with us on scouting-parties. He showed none of the arrogance and conceit so common to British officers, and appeared to be an apt, quick scholar.

Lord Howe

Rogers and Stark were delighted with his military instincts and the keen intelligence with which he made himself master of what was to him a new method of fighting.

When he lived with us, he was as one of us. He washed his own linen at the brook, and ate our coarse fare with his jack-knife. He cut off the skirts of his coat, and had his men do the same, that they might not be impeded by them in the woods. He made them wear leggings and brown the barrels of their guns, that they should not glitter in the sun, and to prevent them from rusting. He had his men cut their hair short, and each of them carried thirty pounds of meal in his knapsack, so that they could go on a long expedition without a wagon-train.

He had great talents as a soldier. Anyone who talked with him felt it at once. And with it all he was simple in his habits and manners, living like one of us, and making his officers lead the same plain life.

The days he spent with the Rangers were days of pride and pleasure to us, for we not only saw his greatness as a soldier, but the bearing of the man was so modest, so genial and lovable, that everyone was greatly attached to him. He liked best of all to talk with John Stark, and to get him to tell of Indians and their habits and ways of fighting. And here he showed his keen insight. For Captain Stark was the best man in the Rangers. Rogers got the credit for what the Rangers did. But much of their success was due to Stark. He was a man whose judgment was sure, who did not make mistakes.

After our defeat in March, Rogers went to Albany to see about getting recruits. While there he was given his commission as Major of the Corps of Rangers.

On the way from Concord to Fort Edward he became well acquainted with Edmund, whose business-like ways and attention to details pleased Rogers so much that when he was made major he appointed Edmund adjutant of the Rangers—a very responsible position for so young a man. It was his duty to record the paroles and countersigns, the various orders for the next day, and to see that they were attended to.

The Provincial Levies

In May the new provincial troops began to come in. We had been long enough in the army to become disciplined, though not in the manner that the regulars were, and had grown accustomed to seeing regiments dressed in uniforms; so that when the new levies came in, we felt some of the amusement of the regulars at their green and awkward ways. Gathered together from country villages, they came in the clothes they wore at home, and put me in mind of Falstaff's soldiers. Some wore long coats, some short coats, and some no coats at all. All the colors of the rainbow were there. Some wore their hair cropped close. Others had their hair done up in cues, and every man in authority wore a wig. All kinds of wigs could be seen—little brown wigs and great, full-bottomed wigs hanging down over their shoulders.

But they were a sturdy set. When you looked at each of them, you saw a man used to hard work from boyhood, more or less accustomed to the woods, and almost without exception a fair shot. Handsome is as handsome does. As the war went on, the regulars found that the rabble were as brave as themselves, more expert in wood-fighting, and far better shots.

But the ridicule that was heaped upon them at first caused a bitter feeling which lasted and prepared the way for the Revolution.

Toward the end of May, it was evident that the army would soon make an advance on the enemy; for everyone was called in, and no furloughs were granted.

We had by this time a great army of nine thousand provincial troops, six thousand regulars, and six hundred Rangers. Many of the regulars were old veterans from European battlefields; and we had not the least doubt but that, when we started, we should go straight through to Canada. Montcalm's little army of thirty-five hundred men at Ticonderoga could offer but slight resistance.

Scouting Parties

Several scouting-parties from the Rangers were sent out to inspect Ticonderoga, and capture prisoners in order to get information from them.

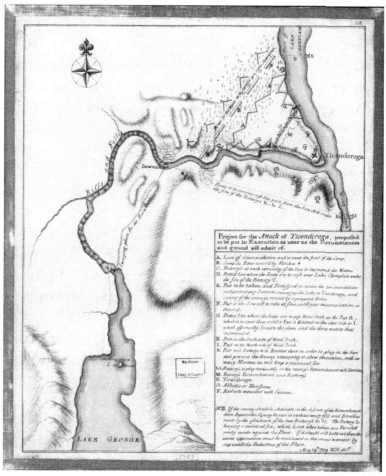

Stark went through the woods to the west of Ticonderoga and brought back six prisoners. Captain Jacobs, with some of his

Indians, went down the east side of Lake Champlain. He had a fight with some of the French, and returned with ten prisoners and seven scalps. Rogers, with our party, went through the woods until we were opposite Crown Point, where we had a little fight and killed one Frenchman, and captured three, whom we brought back.

At the end of May, Lord Howe sent fifty of us under Rogers to inspect the landing-place at the lower end of Lake George, and to make a map of it. We were also to report upon the paths to Ticonderoga, and to find out the number of the French army.

We went down the lake in boats, and while some of the officers were making plans, the rest of us proceeded toward Ticonderoga. We marched, as usual, in single file, along the path we had taken in our trip in March.

Amos said, "I have no p-pleasant recollection of this place, and feel as if we should have some more b-bad luck."

Rogers halted us and went forward with three men, to take a look at the fort. As he was returning, a large party of the enemy set upon us, and we had a lively fight.

Captain Jacob ran off with his Indians, crying out to us: "Come on! Follow me! No good stay here. Heap French! Heap Injun!"

"That's Injun all over," said Martin. "If he gets the upper hand, he'll fight like fury. But if the odds are against him, he'll run like a deer."

We got behind trees and logs, and kept the enemy back. Rogers came round through the woods; and as the attention of the enemy was given entirely to us, he and his party made a rush and joined us.

The enemy had us pretty well surrounded, but we broke through them, losing eight men. We rallied at our boats, and returned home.

The Army Embarks for Ticonderoga

By the 28th of June the whole army under General Abercrombie had arrived at Lake George. A great deal of time seemed to be wasted. But on the 5th of July the whole army of nearly sixteen thousand men embarked in boats and batteaux (*flat-bottomed boat*) for Ticonderoga. The advanced guard was up and out on the lake before daylight—the light infantry on the right, our Rangers on the left, and Colonel Bradstreet's batteaux men in the center.

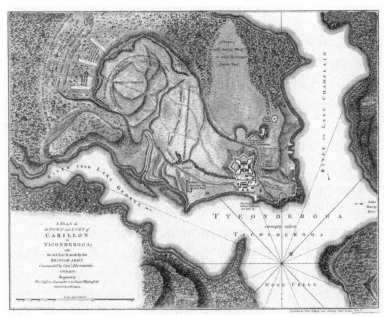

Then came the main body of the army—the provincials, dressed in blue with red facings, on the right and left wings. In the center were the regulars, in scarlet with white facings, and the 42d Regiment, the Black Watch, in kilts and tartans. Behind them came the rear guard of provincials.

Ben Comee; *A True Tale of Rogers's Rangers* 1758-59

The whole army was on the lake as the sun rose, breaking up the mist on the hillsides. The lake was calm and without a ripple.

It was a sight I shall never forget,—the beautiful lake covered by over a thousand boats, the various colored uniforms, the gun-barrels glittering in the sun, the flags of the different regiments, the bagpipes and bands playing, the pretty islands, the green hills and mountains, the mist rising and floating away.

The army rowed until twilight, when we reached Sabbath Day Point, where we rested and ate some food; at ten we started again, and at daybreak the Rangers reached the lower part of the lake. We landed, and received orders from Captain Abercrombie, one of the general's aides-de-camp, to gain the top of a mountain a mile from the landing, and from there to march east to the river that flows into the falls, and get possession of some rising ground there. When we had done this, we were to wait for the army to come up. In an hour's time we got to the rising ground, and found quite a large body of French in front of us. We waited for further orders.

At noon some provincial troops under Colonels Fitch and Lyman came up. And while Rogers was talking to them we heard a sharp firing in the rear of these troops.

Rogers led us round to the left, and we met a force of the enemy who were fighting our men, and had thrown them into confusion. We engaged with them, and killed many. Lord Howe, with Major Israel Putnam and his men, came up on the other side of the French, who were thus surrounded, and almost all of them were killed or captured.

Lord Howe's Death

It was a party of some four hundred Canadians, who had been sent out to watch us, and though they were good woodsmen, they had lost their way in the dense forest, and had wandered into the middle of our army.

There seemed to be a great commotion among Lord Howe's men. I ran over to them with Captain Stark; and there we saw Lord Howe stretched out on the ground—dead.

John Stark is not a man easily stirred. I remember at the battle of Bunker's Hill, when a man rushed up to him, and told him that his son was killed,—which was a mistake, for he is alive at this day,—John turned to the man and said, "Back to your post. This is no time to think of our private affairs."

But when he saw that brilliant soldier, that man whose virtues, accomplishments, and genial, lovable nature showed us what a man might be, lying there, dead, he knelt down beside him, and the tears ran down his cheeks. All of us were overcome with grief, we loved the man so much.

Stark took his hand, bent over, and kissed his forehead.

"Goodbye, my dear friend. God bless you and have mercy on us." He rose, and I walked away with him.

"Comee, the life is departed out of Israel. I have no further faith in this expedition. Our sun is set."

We mourned his loss a long time, and our Province raised the money for a great monument, which was erected to him in Westminster Abbey, in memory of "the affection her officers and soldiers bore to his command."

After Lord Howe was killed, everything fell into disorder. The army became all mixed up in the thick woods, and was sent back to the landing-place.

Chapter XI: Fort Ticonderoga and the Assault

The following morning the Rangers were sent to the front, to the place we occupied the day before. Captain Stark with Captain Abercrombie and Mr. Clark, the engineer, went with two hundred Rangers to Rattlesnake Hill to reconnoiter the French works.

Fort Ticonderoga was at the southern end of the narrow strip of land which lies between Lake Champlain and the outlet of Lake George. A half-mile to the north of the fort, a little ridge runs across the peninsula. As we looked down from the hill, we saw the French hard at work on a strong breastwork of logs which they had nearly completed. At either end of it was low, marshy ground, difficult to pass. The breastwork zigzagged along the ridge in such a manner that if troops attacked it, the French could rake them with grapeshot, and it was too high to climb over.

"How are we going to get over that breastwork, Edmund? There's no slope to it, and we can't reach within two feet of the top."

"Oh, we'll knock it to pieces with cannon, and then we can rush over it. Our officers will know what to do."

"There won't be any rushing through that mass of sharpened stakes that they have driven into the ground in front of the works."

"No. That's so. There's a regular thicket of them with the points sticking out toward us. They'll have to be cut off or torn up, and the French will be raking us all the time."

"See those Canadians cutting down the forest just beyond the stakes. The tops of the trees fall outward, and the branches are matted together. If Abercrombie thinks his army can march up to the breastwork, he's greatly mistaken."

"Yes; it will be a piece of work to scramble through those branches; and then comes the obstacle of stakes; and then a wall eight feet high. Montcalm knows his business, Ben. I wish he were on our side. We shall have no easy task. It looks tough today, and it will be worse tomorrow."

They Inspect Ticonderoga

"We shall lose a good many men. Possibly we may go through the swamp, at the ends of the breastwork."

"Where's Amos?"

We looked round and saw Amos, with his back turned toward us. He seemed deeply interested.

"What is it, Amos? What are you looking at?"

"I tell you, boys, I think this hill's about the best place for p-pigeons I ever saw. There's a good spot for a booth, and that little tree would make a fine standard for a p-pigeon p-pole."

"Hang your pigeons! You may be dead tomorrow. Look down the lake, Edmund. See the reinforcements of French regulars with their white coats rowing up Champlain. They'll be at Fort Ti in half an hour."

We were told to get ready to go back. I overheard Mr. Clark say:—

"Oh, we can take a place like that by an assault with small arms. We'll give them a taste of the bayonet. We don't need cannon."

Stark replied: "I don't think so. Bring some cannon up here, and you can rake the breastwork and drive them out; or take cannon round in front, and you can knock the breastwork to pieces in half an hour, and then you can easily take the place by assault; but otherwise you cannot."

"Oh, I assure you, my dear sir, we can carry a place like that by an assault easily. You provincials have no idea what British officers and British regulars can do."

"I know what Braddock did," said Stark.

We came down the mountain and joined the rest of the Rangers. Stark went with Clark to report to General Abercrombie. He returned and said that Abercrombie had agreed with Clark on an attack with small arms only.

"Tomorrow you'll see a sad sight. You'll see the finest army there ever was in America killed off by the stupidity of its commanding officer. Why couldn't poor Lord Howe have been spared two days longer, to win everlasting renown? We talked this over as we lay on our bearskins at Sabbath Day Point; and if he were alive, there would be no such tomfoolery and murder."

The Army Advances

We lay down in the woods by the river, and slept on our arms. The sun rose the next morning clear and bright. We received orders to advance. We crept through the forest until we came to the open place, where the great trees lay on the ground with their tops toward us.

About two hundred of the French were concealed in the mass of boughs, and fired at us. We got behind trees and logs and returned their fire.

Bradstreet's batteaux men now formed on our left, Gage's light infantry on our right, and three regiments of provincials came up behind us. We exchanged a scattering fire with the enemy. Then we pushed into the mass of boughs and drove the French back into their breastwork.

Colonel Haldiman and the grenadiers now came up in solid formation. We separated and let them pass. They struggled through the trees. The Highlanders of the Black Watch followed them; and I caught sight of Hector, as he went by us, looking very grim and determined. I waved my cap at him, but he was too intent on the work ahead to see me.

What a jaunty, ugly, devil-may-care set of fellows they were! Their uniforms set off their figures to advantage. Their faces showed they were eager for the fight. Their bayonets were fixed, for they had been ordered to take the works by a bayonet charge. When they got through the trees, their formation was completely broken up; but they advanced to the obstacle of sharpened stakes, and were met by a terrible fire of grape and musket shot that mowed them down. They stood at the obstacle, hacking away at the stakes, falling in heaps before the shower of grapeshot. They took off their bayonets and fired at the enemy. Some got through the obstacle, and went up to the breastwork, eight feet high. They tried to scale it, but could not. Unwilling to retreat, they stood in front of it, exchanging shots with the French, shaking their guns at them, and cursing them in Gaelic.

The Regulars Repulsed

"They're b-brave enough, Ben, and hang on like bulldogs; but they can't get over that b-breastwork, unless they grow a couple of feet in a m-mighty short time."

We watched this attack with great interest, for we had wonderful expectations as to what the regulars would do; and they had ridiculed the provincials and lauded themselves so long, that their confidence became unbounded. How they were to take the breastwork in this way, we could not see. But we waited in the hope of seeing the impossible occur. At last the few who were left were driven back.

As they returned, we saw Hector supporting his brother Donald. We ran out from the fallen trees, and helped him through the branches.

"'Deed, man, that was the hottest place I ever was in, and I'm well out of it with naught but a bit of lead in my leg. I dinna envy the poor fellows who have to go in there again."

After this attack there was a lull. Abercrombie, who was in a safe place two miles away, ordered another attack. Some of the provincial regiments were with them. They rushed into the space, like so many cattle into an enclosure, where they were knocked over without a chance to get at their enemy.

We were eager for the Rangers to join in this assault, and asked: "Why don't we advance?" "Why doesn't Rogers order us to attack?" "We ought to help those men and be in the thick of the fight."

Old McKinstry said, "Don't you see, boys, why we don't advance? Because it's all nonsense and folly. We have no orders to go ahead, and Rogers knows it's nothing but murder to put us up before that wall to be shot down. We're doing the best work where we are. See me take off that officer with the white coat." He fired, and the officer fell back. "There, if you can knock over three or four of them, you've done your share."

"He's right, after all, Ben. We're killing more men by picking them off than the regulars are."

They Rescue a Brave Man

I felt easier in my mind after this talk. We stood among the branches, and fired at the heads that appeared above the breastwork.

These assaults were kept up all the afternoon. At five the most determined one took place, and some of the Highlanders succeeded in getting over the breastwork, only to be immediately bayoneted. Colonel Campbell was killed in the fort, and Major Campbell was badly wounded.

While this attack on the right was going on, we saw a provincial who had crept close to the breastwork, and was picking off the Frenchmen.

He was seen by them, and a man fired and wounded him. But he jumped up and brained the man with his hatchet. Then he fell down. It was a pity to let such a brave man lie there to be killed and scalped by the Indians.

I turned to Edmund and said, "Can't we get that man out of there?"

"I will do what you will."

I shouted to our men to cover us as well as they could by their fire, and we ran forward.

The Rangers advanced a little, and opened fire at every head that showed above the breastwork.

Edmund and I got through the obstacle and ran up to the wall. We joined hands. The man sat on them, put his arms around our necks, and we ran off with him.

Some of the enemy fired at us, but the Highlanders were taking most of their attention, and our men were good marksmen, so that but few showed their heads above the breastwork. Still, the bullets whistled about us in a most uncomfortable manner.

We found that the man we had saved was a Rhode Island provincial, named William Smith. He was boiling over with wrath against the French, swore at them like a pirate, and though badly wounded would have crept back if we had not prevented him.

Amos listened to him with wonder, and said, "Your f-friend Smith, Ben, couldn't have b-been raised when there were tithingmen, or he'd have just lived in the stocks. He must have great natural g-gifts to be able to swear like that."

"Here come the regulars again."

A Panic

They passed through the fallen trees, marched up to the breastwork, and again made an attempt to scale it. The French raked them with grapeshot, and soon they came running back nearly frantic with fear. We let them pass and gazed at them with astonishment.

"That's human nature, boys," said McKinstry. "Those men have fought here for six hours, a foolish, hopeless battle. They hung to it like bulldogs. No men could have been braver. All of a sudden the idea strikes them that they are beaten, and they run away in a panic. It's strange. It's mighty strange, but it's human nature."

Rogers shouted: "Stay where you are, boys. Hold your ground and keep on firing."

The Rangers and provincials remained among the fallen trees, exchanging shots with the enemy until dusk. Then we went up to the obstacle and picked out some of the wounded from among the heaps of dead men. This was the hardest part of the day for me, stumbling over the dead, picking up the poor wounded fellows and hearing them moan and cry as we carried them off.

Chapter XII: The Fight at Fort Anne, and the Escape of Amos

When night came on, we retreated with the wounded we had saved. The next morning the whole army re-embarked and rowed up Lake George to the ruins of Fort William Henry and landed. This time we were not admiring the beauty of the scene. We were filled with sorrow and dismay at the failure of the expedition and our terrible disaster. We lost nearly two thousand men. The French lost only about three hundred.

The whole army, regulars and provincials, were indignant with our cowardly and incompetent general, Abercrombie, or Mrs. Nabby Crombie, as the soldiers nicknamed him. We knew that the battle had been badly conducted. We wished to have the cannon brought to the front to batter down the breastworks, and were willing and eager to fight again. But Abercrombie began to entrench, and sent most of his artillery to Albany, lest it should fall into the hands of the enemy.

The Rangers Sent Against the Enemy

The Rangers heard little of this grumbling and dissatisfaction; for as soon as we returned from Ticonderoga we were sent out scouting near the south end of Lake Champlain, and very nearly fell into the hands of a large force of French and Indians. Fortunately we saw them in time to escape.

A few days later, a wagon train was attacked and one hundred and seventy-six men were killed, of whom sixteen were Rangers. The news of this disaster came in the night, and at two in the morning Rogers started out with a large party of regulars, provincials, and Rangers to head off the enemy. We rowed down

Lake George at the top of our speed, and then marched over the mountain to the narrow waters of Lake Champlain. But though we made all possible haste, so did the enemy, and we missed them by a couple of hours.

We rested for a time; for we were much exhausted by our efforts, and were about to march back, when a messenger arrived, who gave us orders to go to Fort Anne at Wood Creek, and cut off a party of French and Indians who were near Fort Edward.

We had about five hundred men, eighty of whom were Rangers. The rest was made up of some of Gage's light infantry and Connecticut troops, under Major Israel Putnam.

On the 7th of August we reached the spot where old Fort Anne had stood, and camped there.

The forest for a mile around the old fort had been cut down and burned years before. But the fort had rotted away, and the clearings had become overgrown with bushes, with here and there an open space.

Early the next morning we began our march. Putnam and his men were in front, the light infantry in the center, and the Rangers in the rear.

Rogers had been shooting at a mark that morning with Lieutenant Irwin of the regulars. The enemy had overheard the firing and ambushed us.

Putnam was leading his men. As he left the clearing, and entered the forest, the yelling and firing began. Several Indians rushed at him. His gun missed fire, and he with three or four men was captured by the Indians.

Ben Wrestles with an Indian

The redskins forced the Connecticut men back, the light infantry held their ground, and we of the Rangers struggled through the bushes as best we could, to get to the front.

Every one fought for himself. I had fired my gun just as I reached an open space, and seeing a number of men on the other side, I started to run across to them.

Of course I should have reloaded before I attempted this; but one does not always do the right thing, especially in a hot fight. I had gone but a short distance when an Indian fired at me from the bushes, and then ran at me with a tomahawk.

I turned, parried the blow with my gun, and the tomahawk was struck from his hand.

We grappled each other. He was a fine, large man, decked out with feathers and war paint, and was the strongest and most active man I ever got hold of. He seemed to be made of steel springs. As I struggled with him, I couldn't help thinking, "What a splendid wrestler you would make if you only knew the tricks!" I gave him Jonas Parker's best throw, and we came down together, and I on top.

The fall knocked the wind out of him and partly stunned him. I got hold of my hatchet and brained him. I had not noticed or thought of anything but him. But now I heard a crack! crack! zip! zip!

As I started to run I felt a pain in my left arm, and also in my left leg. But I got off to our men among the bushes, and they bound my arm up, and put a bandage round my leg.

I saw an Indian leap in among the regulars, and kill two men with his hatchet. Then he jumped on a log and taunted our men. A soldier struck at him with his gun and made him bleed. The Indian was returning the blow with his tomahawk, when Rogers shot him.

I was still able to load and shoot. We fought some two hours before they gave way. At last they broke up into little parties and ran off. We remained and buried our dead.

Ben Wounded

We lost about fifty men. The French and Indians left over one hundred dead on the field; and their loss was much heavier, for they carried off most of their dead.

My wounds now made me so lame and stiff that I could not walk, and was carried on a litter of branches.

Rogers came alongside, and said, "That was a mighty pretty wrestle, Comee. Big stakes up too; glad you won. But I believe if that Indian had been taught the tricks like a Christian, you would have met your match."

"That's just what I was thinking myself, major, all the time I was wrestling with him. It's an awful pity to have to kill a man like that."

"Oh, pshaw, nothing but a cussed redskin. That makes one less of the vermin. All of us on both sides round that clearing watched you and him, and did not pay much attention to each other until it was over. When you killed him, and got up, they fired at you, and we began to fire at them again. But for a short time all of us watched you. He must have been a big Injun among them."

"Major, where is Amos Locke?"

"I don't know. I don't think he was among the killed or wounded; and if he isn't with our party here, he's probably a prisoner, perhaps roasted and scalped by this time."

Edmund came up later. "I'm afraid, Ben, we shan't see Amos again. He and I were together for a while. But in running through the bushes we got separated, and I can't find him among our men. If he were with our party, he would have come to us by this time."

"Poor fellow! I can't bear to think of him in the woods, dead; or worse still, being tortured by the Indians. He may turn up again, after all."

When we arrived at camp at Lake George, we found that it had been strongly entrenched.

The camp was dirty and filthy, particularly the portion occupied by the provincials, for our officers were ignorant in such matters.

On the way to and from Ticonderoga the men had drunk a good deal of lake water, and this with the grief over our defeat and the filthy state of our camp had caused much sickness.

Provincials Beat Regulars Shooting

Having been out in the woods on scouts, I was in good condition, and my wounds began to heal quickly. Edmund took me over to see the man we had rescued at Ticonderoga. We found him doing well, cursing the French, and aching to get at them again. We looked up our kinsmen Hector and Donald and struck up a great friendship with the men of the Black Watch. Hector and Donald were both God-fearing men, and went with us several times to hear Parson Cleveland of Bagley's regiment preach. He gave us sermons full of meat, and we enjoyed them.

The regulars and provincials did not get on well together. The Englishmen looked down on the provincial officers and men, and this caused much hard feeling. One day in August, the regulars and provincials practiced firing with great guns at a target in the lake, and our men beat the regulars thoroughly. That pleased us and made the old country men feel pretty glum. Although the regulars scorned the provincials, yet they held the Rangers in high esteem.

"Why is it, Donald," I asked, "that the regulars think so well of us, and laugh at the rest of the provincials?"

"Well, man, one reason is, because you're no province soldiers at all, being in the direct pay and service of the King, like ourselves. And then you're a braw set of men, and ken this fighting in the woods a deal better than we do, and we know it. But the provincials are gawks from country towns, without discipline, and with no more knowledge of the woods than we have."

"But Edmund and I are from a town like them."

"You've keppit gude company, since you've been with the Rangers, and have been long enough with them to look and act like the rest of them. One would take you for hunters and woodsmen."

"But the provincials were the last to leave the field at Ticonderoga."

"I'm no denying it. They fought well."

"And for country greenhorns, they did pretty well with the cannon the other day."

"Aye, man, I'm no saying they didn't. I'm a truthful man, and I maun say I was sair disappointed when they beat us shooting." And he changed the subject.

Lake George

Though our camp was foul, yet the lake was the fairest spot I have ever seen—dotted with islands and hemmed in by mountains. Even Hector and Donald said it was "a bonny place, just for all the world like old Scotland."

We used to row on the lake, among the pretty islands, or lie in the boat and gaze at the mountains and the clouds floating over them. It seemed absurd that two great bodies of men should come to such a serene, peaceful place, and occupy their time killing each other.

About two weeks after the Fort Anne fight, Edmund and I had a chance to get away from camp for several hours, and started off with 'Bijah Thompson of Woburn, whom we found in Colonel Nichols's regiment.

We pulled out on the lake, went in swimming, and then rowed slowly along with our fish-lines trailing behind. But the fish didn't bite. We cut across the upper part of the lake, and as we approached the further side, Edmund said, "What's that over on the shore, Ben? There's someone there who seems to be making motions to us."

We rowed in that direction, and saw a man waving his arms, and heard a "hello!"

"That's no Frenchman. That's one of our men who has got lost in the woods, or who has escaped from the French."

As we came nearer, we saw that he was almost naked. We pulled toward the shore, and beheld a pitiful, haggard fellow, with nothing on him but a pair of ragged breeches and a tattered shirt. We were about to ask him some questions, when he exclaimed:—

"B-B-Ben and Edmund, and 'B-Bijah Thompson too, by gum! An-An-And ain't I glad to see you?"

"Amos Locke! And we're glad to see you, too. Where have you been?"

"B-Been? I've been in h-hell. Say, have you got anything to eat? I'm starved."

We had a lot of rye and Injun bread, cheese, and boiled beef with us. We brought it out, and Amos gulped away at it like a hungry dog. We also had a wooden bottle into which we had poured our rations of rum, and then filled it up with water. We passed it to Amos, and he took a long swig at it. As he took it away from his mouth, a happy grin came over his face.

Amos Comes Back

"B-Boys, that goes to the spot. I'm not a rum-drinker, but when a fellow's been frozen, and starved, and water-logged, he does sort of hanker after something that has a t-tang to it."

He put down the bottle, and went to work at the food again. In a short time our lunch had disappeared—and we had put up what we considered was an ample supply for three hearty men.

I picked up my jacket and handed it to him to put on; for though it was a warm day, he looked cold and peaked. His feet were badly cut, and were done up in bandages of cloth. Then I filled my pipe, and taking out my flint and steel, lit it and gave it to him.

"This isn't b-bad. Now row to the place where the victuals (*provisions*) are."

Edmund and 'Bijah rowed, while I questioned Amos.

"Well, I was running through the b-bushes, just a little behind you, Edmund, when my foot caught in a root or vine, and over I went ker-flummux. My gun flew out of my hands, and as I was g-getting up, two Frenchmen grabbed me and p-pulled me off through the woods. When they had gone quite a distance, they t-tied me to a tree, and went back to fight. I heard the firing and tried to get loose, but couldn't.

"A young Injun came along and had some f-fun throwing his tomahawk at the tree, just over my head, seeing how near he could come to it without hitting me.

"After he had done this half a dozen times, he stood in front of me, and said, 'Ugh! Me big Injun.' I said, 'Yes, you big Injun. Big Injun better go fight.' He went away, and in about an hour my two Frenchmen came running back with more men. They untied me, and fastening a line around my neck, one led and the other drove me, hitting me with his loaded gun, punching the muzzle into my b-back. When they got to the place where they had left their packs, they p-pulled off my jacket and waistcoat, t-tied a heavy pack on my back, and drove me along again.

Israel Putnam has a Warm Time

"Every now and then I sank down, and thought I c-couldn't go any further; but the man behind put his gun to my head, r-r-ripped out a lot of oaths at me, and told me he would blow my head off if I didn't get up and hustle.

"Oh, no, I don't know their lingo; but I could understand just what he said, and what's m-more, I know he m-meant it. I didn't want to be a c-cold corpse out there in the woods, so I got up and struggled on again.

"At last they camped for the night. They laid me on my back and t-tied my hands and feet to stakes d-driven into the ground.

"I saw Major P-Putnam, who had been captured by some Injuns. They took his pack off, and he looked as if he would drop. They r-rushed at him, stripped him, t-tied him to a tree, piled dry branches and brush about him, and set them on fire. Then they formed a ring around him, and taunted and insulted him. A shower came up and put the fire out. They g-got more branches and lighted the fire again. The fire was burning well, and P-Putnam was squirming away from the heat, when a French officer ran up, k-kicked the branches aside, cut the cords, told the Injuns to stand back, and led P-Putnam away. I heard afterward that this man's name was Morin, and that he was the leader of the expedition.

"The next morning at daybreak we got into the b-batteaux and canoes, and rowed down Wood Creek. I was in a b-batteau. They gave me an oar, and made me work for all I was worth. If I let up for a minute, they hit me and threatened to k-kill me. That ugly fellow who swore at me the day before was in the boat, and I c-could understand him. He made things very clear, as he jabbed the m-muzzle of his gun into my ribs, and h-held his finger on the trigger.

"They were in a hurry to get out of the way of any f-force of our men that might be sent to cut them off. We reached T-Ticonderoga that night. They turned us prisoners out into a pasture with some scrubby trees in it, and p-put a guard around us. And there they k-kept us, giving us hardly anything to eat, until at last we grew so hungry that we p-pulled the bark off the b-black birches, and ate it to stay our stomachs. I thought considerable of home while I was b-browsing round in that p-pasture, and of what I used to do. Not so m-much of pigeon-shooting and fox hunting as of things I disliked, p-ploughing in the spring, hilling corn until my back ached, cutting logs into lengths for firewood until my arms were t-tired out and my hands b-blistered.

Fond Recollections

"These were all unpleasant, but I remembered the comfortable home and the supper that came after the work, and how I used to eat my fill in safety. And here I was, likely to be scalped or burned to death, and my innards just a griping and a yearning for a b-bit of solid food.

"There were some four thousand Frenchmen in the fort, Canadians, Indians, and the regulars in their white coats.

"I was bound to get away if I could, and watched for a chance. We were not f-far from the breastwork.

"Sentinels walked up and down on the inner side, and I knew that I could not c-crawl over it, without being seen. They did not pay so much attention to the swampy ground at either end. I made up my mind to g-get to the low land, and pass by the end of the breastwork.

"After we had been there six days, a storm began in the afternoon. The rain came down in torrents, and the wind b-blew hard.

"We were out in the wet, soaking. When the French had gone to sleep, I walked to the f-fence which was round our pasture, and waited for the sentinel to pass. Then I crept under the fence, and crawled along until I got to the swamp, and went into the edge of it and walked toward the end of the breastwork. The f-fall of rain had made the swamp worse than usual.

"As I walked along in the mire, I felt that I was sinking, and caught hold of a t-tree and pulled myself out, but left my shoes behind. Then I kept close to the edge of the swamp, and went along carefully, t-till I got near the breastwork.

A Stroll Through the Woods

"I heard the sentinel c-coming my way, and lay down until he t-turned and walked away from me.

"I passed by the end of the breastwork, and kept along the edge of the forest, t-till I felt there was an opening, which I knew must be the path we travelled over on our way from Lake George. It was blind going, p-pitch dark. Every now and then I found myself wandering from the path, b-but luckily the passage of our large army had t-trodden it down into a road, so that I k-kept my way, though it was with great d-difficulty.

"As it began to grow light, I reached a point where a ledge came down to the road; and I thought this would be a good place to leave the path, because if the Indians searched for me, they would lose my trail on the r-rocks.

"I walked on the rocks for over an hour, t-till the sun rose, and the rain ceased. I came across a blueberry patch, and ate my fill. It was good to be free and to have something to eat.

"I found a hollow where I would not be seen, and where the sun would shine on me, and I lay down and slept. When I w-woke up, and was thinking what to do, a rabbit came hopping along, feeding. I kept quiet until he had passed me, and rose up and c-cried out, Hooh! He sat up on his hind legs, pricked up his ears, and I knocked him over with a stone and ate him. Then I came to the brook where we had our f-first fight, but it was so full from the rain that I had to wait a day before I could cross it. It ran like a m-mill-race. My feet were all cut up, and I tore off the arms of my shirt and bound the cloth round my feet. I didn't d-dare to follow the paths, but kept through the woods t-till I struck the lake. I only travelled in the morning and afternoon, for when the sun was overhead I c-couldn't tell where I was going; so I ate berries and slept at midday. I reached the lake above the Narrows and went back to the path. I didn't care m-much if I were caught or not. I don't want to eat another b-berry in my life. Several times I saw boats on the lake and tried to get their attention, but c-couldn't. D-Didn't I feel happy when I saw you coming toward me! And when

I knew who it was, I felt as if I were at home again m-milking the cows or up on old B-Bull Meadow shooting fifty-two pigeons at a clip. Have you heard anything from Davy Fiske?"

News from Weaver David

"Well, yes; 'Bijah here came out late, and he says Davy has been telling him some story about killing a bear in Grimes's cornfield up on the Billerica road."

"That must have b-been before we left and we didn't hear anything about it. How was it, 'Bijah?"

"I met Davy early this spring over in the woods by Listening Hill, and he told me about hunting a bear in Bill Grimes's young corn, which was about three feet high. He and Bill chased the bear; the bear ran off, climbed over a stone wall, and got stuck in a snowdrift, and they came up and killed him."

"That's D-Davy all over. He's m-mighty careless about those hunting yarns of his. Pretty soon the bears will be wearing rackets in the summer to k-keep out of his way. And now, boys, if you don't mind, I'll stretch out in the bottom of the boat and get a little nap. I haven't had a good sleep I don't know when, and the f-food and the warm sun make me terrible sleepy."

Amos lay down, and we rowed until we reached the shore.

Chapter XIII: Ben Comee Heap Big Paleface—Trapping Bobcats in Primeval Woods

When we arrived at camp we had something to eat. Rogers came to us and questioned Amos, first as to the number of troops at Fort Ticonderoga, and how they were arranged, and afterward he inquired about his adventures. When Amos told how Morin rushed in and freed Major Putnam, Rogers said,—

"Morin? I know him well. I scalped him and carved my name on his breast with my knife."

"Well, I wished you h-hadn't. Then he m-might have given us something to eat."

Rogers turned and went off.

"Ugh! I don't like that man. You remember the time Lord Howe was k-killed. Well, that day I saw Rogers hit a poor wounded Frenchman on the head with his hatchet. It was the meanest thing I ever saw done by a white man, and I can't abide him."

"No, he's cruel and hard as nails. I wish John Stark was the commander of the Rangers. He has all Rogers's good points as a fighter, is a better man, and has better judgment. He never makes mistakes."

"Hello!" said Amos. "There's old Captain Jacob. I thought I'd n-never want to see an Injun again. But it's kind of good to see the old fellow. I wonder what makes him seem different from the Injuns on the other side."

"Probably because he's a Christian Indian."

"I guess not. I d-don't think his religion struck in very deep, and it don't worry him much. And when you come to that, they say those French Indians are Christian Indians too. I n-never noticed m-much religion about them. I guess we like him because he's on our side and shows his good points to us, and those other Injuns are agin us and show their ugly natures. It makes all the difference in the world whether the Injun's with you or agin you."

Ben Sends Presents

I had been feeling bad about the Indian that I wrestled with. He was such a fine fellow. How Jonas Parker would have delighted in him. Just a bundle of steel springs. There must have been a great deal that was good in a man like that.

I walked over to Captain Jacob, and said, "I had a wrestle with an Indian in that Fort Anne fight, Captain Jacob, and I killed him. I'm sorry, for he was a fine fellow."

"Yes, I heard! Big fight. Big Injun."

"Well, I should like to show those Indians that I thought well of him, and want also to do something for his wife and children, if he has any. Now, I have ten Spanish dollars. I should like to buy some present, and send it to them, and tell them how much I thought of him and that I'm sorry I killed him."

"Oh, yes! Me send Injun. Me send what you call 'em—Injun flag of truce. Me send presents. Tell 'em you heap sorry. Me tell 'em you think him heap big Injun."

"That's it. That's the talk, Captain Jacob. Here's the ten dollars. Buy what you think are the right presents for his wife and children, and I shall be much obliged to you."

"All right! Me do it!"

Some days later, Captain Jacob came to me and said,—

"All right, Ben Comee. Me send Injun. He see them Injuns. He give 'em your words. Injuns feel heap proud. They say that Injun, him big chief of Canawaugha Injuns. His name Gray Wolf. Best man they have. They feel glad you think heap of him. My Injun give 'em presents for his squaw and children. Give 'em rum, tobacco, and chocolate."

"Rum, tobacco, and chocolate?"

"Yes, heap rum, heap tobacco, heap chocolate!"

"Well, that was a mighty good idea, Jacob. There's lots of comfort in all three of those things. But I should never have thought of giving them to the widow and the orphans."

"Injuns ask, 'What that man's name?' 'Ben Comee in Captain Rogers's company. They give my Injun, pipe, wampum, and powder horn with carving on it for you.' They say: 'Ben Comee heap big paleface to kill Gray Wolf. We think as much of his scalp as of Captain Rogers's or John Stark's.'"

Louisburg Falls

Edmund and Amos, who were standing nearby, grinned, and Edmund said,—

"You seem to be pretty popular with those Indians, Ben. Don't get stuck-up over it."

"I don't see anything very funny about it, and hope that all three of us shall pass through the fiery furnace, like Shadrach, Meshach, and Abednego, without a hair of our heads being touched."

While we were being whipped by the French at Ticonderoga, another army under General Amherst and General Wolfe was besieging the fortress of Louisburg, on the island of Cape Breton. That army had good generals; and on the 28th of August we heard that the fortress had surrendered. Edmund came out of Rogers's hut. We were waiting for him.

"Come along with me. Louisburg has fallen, and I've got to take some orders to the officers, about tonight. The four companies of Rangers with that army did well. Rogers is mightily pleased over it, and is going to celebrate their good behavior. Rangers to be at the breastworks at six, and fire a salute. There's going to be hijinks tonight. I've got to go in here and see Stark."

The regiments were all under arms at the breastworks at six o'clock. It was the King's birthday, and the Royal Artillery began with a royal salute of twenty-one guns. Then the regiments fired in turn, until all had fired three times. After that the ranks were broken, and the fun began.

More good news came soon after, and this time our own army had a success. For Colonel Bradstreet with two thousand men had set out on an expedition against Fort Frontenac, and early in September he sent back word that he had taken and destroyed the fort.

These victories put new life into our men, and they became cheerful, and did not continually harp on our defeat.

Through Hector and Donald we came to know the men of the Black Watch well, and spent much of our leisure time with them, listening to their tales of cattle-lifting and of fighting in the Border.

Border Tales

Most of their talk was about the Rebellion of 1745, for the regiment was largely made up of Highlanders that had been "out" with Charlie. And when they drank the King's health, it was to King James they drank, and not to King George.

Their conversation was very interesting to Edmund and to me, for our family had lived together like a clan in Lexington, and the older people still kept certain Scotch customs and used queer expressions. As the Highlanders talked, a strange feeling would

Ben Comee; *A True Tale of Rogers's Rangers* **1758-59**　　　　　　　　121 occasionally come over us, as if we had led that life and seen those sights at some dim, remote period.

In our own camp with the Rangers we heard stories of adventures in the woods with Indians, bears, and lucivees (*wildcat spirit*).

Old Bill McKinstry said, "I wish we had some good strong traps, and we could go off and trap bobcat."

"And why shouldn't we have traps? What am I a blacksmith for? Just find me some old iron, and I will get the use of the armorers' forge."

They procured the iron, and I made eight big traps with strong jaws and a chain for each trap.

McKinstry, John Martin, Amos, and I got a furlough for a week, and so did Hector Munro, whom we asked to go with us. We packed up our traps and provisions on an Indian sled.

The winter had set in. The river was frozen over, and the snow was deep. We fastened on our rackets and started to the southwest, where there was little likelihood that we should be disturbed by Indians. We went down the river, and turned off into a path that led to the west, and followed it until well into the afternoon, when we came to a good-sized pond. On the way, we shot several rabbits with which to bait the traps. McKinstry killed a hedgehog, which he said was just what he wanted. We chose a place where there were a couple of good sized saplings, some twelve feet apart in a level and sheltered spot, not far from the pond.

Building a Camp

We cleared away the brush behind them, and fastened a pole from one tree to the other, some eight feet from the ground. Then we cut a number of long poles, and laying one end of them on the cross pole, and the other on the ground, made the skeleton of a lean-to hut. McKinstry had built a fire. He threw the hedgehog into it, and let him stay until the quills were well singed. Then he pulled him out and tied a string to him.

"What are you doing that for?"

"For a scent. I'll show you."

McKinstry and I set out with the traps and bait, leaving our companions to cut fir boughs, with which to thatch the roof and sides of the hut, and make a bed. He held the hedgehog up by the string, and we walked down to the pond, and along the edge of it.

"There's tracks enough, Ben. Must be game here. I'll scoop out a little snow, and you open the trap, and lay it in the hollow. Now, we'll cover it with twigs and leaves, to hide it. Cut up a rabbit, and lay the pieces on the twigs for bait. Bring me that log over there, and I'll fasten it to the chain for a clog. He'd gnaw, or pull his foot off, if we tied the trap to a tree. He'll haul the clog along, but he won't get many miles with it. Now we'll drag the hedgehog round, and the burnt quills will make a strong scent on the snow. That will do. We'll go on and pull the hedgehog through the snow behind us. When the animals strike that trail, they'll be apt to follow it to a trap."

We set all our traps along the edge of the pond, at quite a distance from each other; and at the last trap, cut up the hog, and baited the trap with it.

When we got back to camp, we found the roof and sides of the hut well thatched with boughs, and a good thick layer of them on the ground for a bed. The boys had collected a lot of wood, and piled it up nearby. In front of the hut was a fire, at which Martin was baking some rye and Injun bread, and frying a large mess of pork.

When we had eaten our supper, it was solid comfort to sit in our hut, after our long day's work, to look at the fire blazing in front, to feel the heat, and watch the smoke curl up through the tree. On the further side of the fire they had built up a wall of green logs, so that the heat was thrown into the hut. We were snug and warm.

John McNeil

"Boys," said McKinstry, "when we get through with this war, you must come to the Amoskeag Falls, and visit your old friends. We've got some fine men there,—one's a great wrestler. I don't think your Jonas Parker could have stood up very long against him. His name is John McNeil. He is six feet six inches high, and used to be strong as a bull. He is a North of Ireland man, and had a quarrel with some big Injun over there, who came along on horseback, and struck at him with his whip. John pulled him off his horse, gave him a pounding, and had to leave the country. He settled at the Falls, and no man, white or red, could stand up against him for a minute. His wife, Christie, is a good mate to him, a big, brawny woman. One day a stranger came to the house and asked: 'Is Mr. McNeil at home?'

"'No,' says Christie; 'the gude man is away.'

"'That's a pity; for I hear that McNeil is a very strong man, and a great wrestler; and I've come a very long distance to throw him.'

"'Troth, man,' says she, 'Johnny is gone. But I'm not the woman to see ye disappointed, and I think if ye'll try me, I'll thraw ye myself.'

"The man didn't like to be stumped by a woman and accepted the challenge. Christie threw him, and he cleared out without leaving his name."

"That's a braw couple," says Hector. "I hope there were no quarrels in that household."

"No, indeed; as nice, peaceable, and respectable a couple as you could find in the whole Province. It's a fine sight to see the old man and his wife seated in front of the fire, smoking their pipes, and their big sons around them."

"I'd like to see them. But what I do want to see is a panther or catamount. There's very little game left in Lexington. Now and then a bear, but the catamounts (*large wild cat*) went long before my day. I suppose you have killed them."

A Hazardous Adventure

"Yes, I've killed some; but Martin's brothers did about the best thing in that way that I know of. Tell them about it, Martin."

"All right. We lived on the Merrimac, at a ferry that they called after us, Martin's Ferry. Father died when we were little chaps. Mother was strong, and we got along farming, hunting, and running the ferry. One day in winter, when I was about thirteen years old, my brothers, Nat and Ebenezer, went up to Nott's Brook, to see if they could find some deer yarded in the swamp. They came on a big track, followed it, and saw a catamount eating a deer it had killed. Nat had an axe, and Eben a club. Nat said, 'Let's kill him, Eben.'

"'All right. It's a pretty slim show, but I'm in for it. How'll we do it?'

"'You go up in front of him and shake your club to take his attention, and I'll creep up behind and hit him with the axe.'

"'I don't think there's much fun shaking a club in a panther's face; but if you're sure you'll kill him, I'll try it.'

"Eben walked up in front with his club, and Nat crept up behind. When the cat saw Eben, it growled and switched its tail round, and raised up the snow in little clouds. It lay there with its paws on the deer and its head raised, growling at Eben, who felt pretty shaky. Nat crept up behind the cat and gave it a blow with his axe that cut its backbone in two."

"That was an awful p-plucky thing to do."

"It was a most unfortunate thing for my mother."

"How's that?"

"Why, it made me just wild to go bear hunting with them. I kept plaguing mother to let me go. She used to say, 'Pshaw, boy, you'd run if you saw a bear.' One night I had been pestering her worse than usual. She left the room, and soon after I heard something bumping round outside. The door flew open, and in walked a bear, which came at me, growling. I grabbed a pine knot that was handy and hit the beast on the head, and over it rolled. The bearskin fell off, and there lay my mother stretched out on the floor. I was afraid I had killed her, and ran and got a pail of water and threw it on her. She came to, and sat up in a kind of a daze.

Martin's Mother Played Bear

"'What's the matter? Have I been in the river?'

"'No, mother, you played you was a bear, and I hit you over the head; I'm awful sorry.'

"'Don't say a word more, Johnny. Don't say a word more. I was an old fool. Serves me right.'

"She got up, threw the bearskin in the corner, and went about her work. In the morning I asked her again if I could go bear-hunting with the boys.

"She put her hands on her hips, looked at me, and laughed to herself, and then she said,—

"'Yes, Johnny, you can go. But be sure and take a club with you. I think you'll be a great help.'"

Just as Martin had finished his story we heard a series of the most terrific screeches and caterwauls.

"Heavens and earth, man," said Hector, "what's that? That must be the father of all cats."

"That's just what he is, and you'll think so tomorrow when you see him. That is, if he don't get away. That's what we call a bobcat. The French call them lucivees; and he's the biggest cat in the country, except the catamount. It's just as well to leave him alone over-night. We don't want to go fooling round him in the dark."

"Weel, mon, generally speaking I have nae fear of a cat; but if this one has claws and teeth like his screech, I think we'd better defer our veesit until the morrow. And it's surprising to me how comfortable we all are out here in the forest in the dead of winter. 'Deed, if Donald and I were out here alone, we'd be freezing; and here we are as happy as kings."

"Yes, and a bagpiper at hand with his music."

"Now, Benny, don't run the bagpipes down. They're a grand instrument. Our friend down there does very well in his way; but he hasna the science. And I was thinking that all we'll be wanting is a little gude peat in the fire. The peat makes a bonny fire. We're no so wasteful of wood as you are."

The Laird of Inverawe

"Well, Hector, we burn peat in our fires at Lexington, too."
"Then you're more civilized than I thought."

"Oh, all we really lack are the bagpipes and some of those second-sight men and Scotch ghosts, who foretell what is going to happen. It's strange some of them didn't tell Nabby Crombie he ought to take his cannon with him when he attacked Ticonderoga."

"We kenned more about Ticonderoga than you think, Comee. Didn't every mother's son in the Black Watch know that our major, Duncan Campbell, would meet his death there? He had his warning years ago."

"A wise man don't do anything great if he tells a soldier that he's likely to be killed some time. But as you seem to think there is something remarkable in your story, you'd better give us a few solid facts. We might not look at it just as you do."

"Duncan Campbell was the laird (*land owner*) of Inverawe Castle in the Highlands, and with us was called, from his estate, Inverawe. One evening he heard a knocking at his door, and, opening it, saw a stranger with torn clothes and his hands and kilt smeared with blood. He said that he had killed a man in a quarrel and that men were after him in order to slay him. He asked for shelter. Inverawe promised to conceal him. The man said, 'Swear it on your dirk (*long dagger*),' and Inverawe did so. He hid the man in a secret room in his castle. Soon after there was a knocking at his gate, and two men entered.

"'Your cousin Donald has just been murdered, and we are looking for the murderer.' Inverawe couldn't go back on his oath, and said he kenned naught of the fugitive; and the men kept on in pursuit. He lay down in a dark room, and went to sleep. Waking up, he saw the ghost of his cousin Donald by his bedside, and heard him say:—

"'Inverawe! Inverawe! Blood has been shed. Shield not the murderer.' When the morning came, he went to the man and told him he could conceal him no longer.

"'You have sworn on your dirk,' the man replied. The laird didn't know what to do. He led the man to a mountain, and hid him in a cave, and told him he wouldn't betray him.

Inverawe's Fate Foretold

"The next night his cousin Donald appeared to him again, and said, 'Inverawe! Inverawe! Blood has been shed. Shield not the murderer.'

"When the sun came up, Inverawe went to the cave, but the man was gone. That night the ghost appeared again, a gruesome sight, but not so stern. 'Farewell! Farewell! Inverawe!' it said. 'Farewell until we meet at Ticonderoga.'

"Inverawe joined the Black Watch. They were hunting us down in the Highlands, after we had been out with Charlie. When this war came on, the King granted us a pardon if we would enlist; and right glad we were to get out of the country. We reached here and learned that we were to attack Ticonderoga. All of us knew the story. When we reached there, the officers said, 'This is not Ticonderoga. This is Fort George.' On the morning of the battle, Inverawe came from his tent, a broken man, and went to the officers, ghastly pale. 'I have seen him. You have deceived me. He came to my tent last night. This is Ticonderoga; I shall die today.'"

"But he didn't die that day," said Martin. "He was hit in the arm, and didn't die until ten days after."

"If you're going to split straws about it," said McKinstry, "the ghost didn't tell him he would be killed there. He got his death wound, at any rate; that was near enough. A good deal better guess

Ben Comee; *A True Tale of Rogers's Rangers 1758-59*

than you could make. Between the yelling of that bobcat and Hector's grisly story, we're likely to have a good night's sleep. I think we'd better frighten the ghosts off, and then turn in."

In the morning, Hector, Amos, and I wanted to go to the traps at once to examine them; but Martin said, "It may be hours before we get back, and if you were to start without your breakfast, you might be calling yourselves pretty hard names later in the day."

We cooked breakfast, and after we had eaten it, took our guns, and went to the pond. Our first trap was gone; but there was a big trail where the clog had been dragged through the snow and bushes.

We followed it for nearly half a mile, until Martin stopped us and said, "There he is."

They Kill a Bobcat

We looked into a clump of bushes, and saw a pair of fierce blue eyes, which looked like polished steel. As we gazed, they seemed to grow larger and flash fire.

"'Deed, mon," said Hector, "a more wicked pair of eyes I never saw."

Martin raised his gun and fired at the bobcat; but though he wounded it, the cat jumped at us, pulling the clog after it. McKinstry gave it another shot, which knocked it over. It died hard.

When the animal was dead, we examined it. It was over three feet long and about two feet high. Its tail was about six inches long. Its head was about as big as a half-peck measure. Its ears were pointed, with little black tassels at the ends. It had whiskers on its cheeks and smellers like a cat. The fur was gray, except that on the belly, which was white.

Hector was looking at its claws, which were nearly two inches long.

"McKinstry, what do these animals eat?"

"Well, if you were alone here in the woods, I think likely they'd eat a Scotchman."

"I was a thinking that same thing myself."

We skinned the bobcat, and cut off some of his flesh with which to bait the trap, and then we carried the trap back, and set and baited it again.

We found nothing in our other traps until we came to the spot where the seventh one had been, and that had disappeared.

We followed the trail, and finally saw the cat on a stump among some bushes. McKinstry shot it. It jumped at us, but fell dead.

It was like the other, and weighed something over thirty pounds, though it looked much heavier on account of its long fur.

We skinned it, and set and baited the trap again. The last trap had not been touched.

As we were going back, Amos said, "What a p-pity Davy Fiske c-couldn't have been with us. He'd have talked of this all his life."

"Well, the only difference is, that Amos Locke will, instead."

Just before we left the pond, we saw that an animal had turned in on our tracks, and had followed them up toward the camp.

A Fisher

"That's a black cat or fisher," said Martin. "His tracks look like a little child's. I'd like to get him, for a black cat's fur is worth something."

The tracks kept along with ours, and when we got to the camp, we found that he had eaten up one of three partridges we had left there.

"I'll fix him," said McKinstry, and the next day he brought up a trap and set it near the hut, and baited it with partridge. The following day, while we were away, the black cat came again, passed by our trap and bait, and though there was a fire burning, went to the hut and ate some baked beans which were there. He made two more calls on us, but scorned the trap.

On the second day out, Martin shot a deer, so that we had plenty of fresh meat; and we cut holes in the ice on the pond and caught pickerel.

When the week was up, we had eight bobcats and an otter. We packed our traps and skins on the sled, started back, and reached Fort Edward in the evening.

Edmund had been unable to go with us on this trip, as Major Rogers was at Albany, and Edmund's duties as adjutant kept him in camp.

Chapter XIV: A Scouting Expedition in the Dead of Winter

One day about the end of February, Edmund came out of Rogers's hut, and said,—

"Rogers is going on a scout, boys, down to Ticonderoga, and will take your company. Johnson is going to send over fifty Mohawk Indians under Captain Lotridge, and there'll be a number of regulars, too. There will be about three hundred and fifty men in the party, so that there won't be much chance of your being treated as we were in our first expedition. An engineer lieutenant named Bhreems is going with you, and will make sketches of the fort. You are to try and take some prisoners to bring back information."

We set out on the third of March, 1759.

The snow was deep, and the Rangers and Indians were on snowshoes. The regulars followed us, plodding along heavily through the snow. We reached Halfway Brook that night, and the next day got over to Lake George. We waited until it was dark and then marched down the lake to the First Narrows, which we reached about two in the morning.

It was bitter cold, and already some of the men were so badly frost-bitten that twenty of them had been sent back to Fort Edward.

"Now, boys," said Rogers, "we must keep under cover all day and hide until night comes on. You can't have any fires. Get into sheltered spots and huddle together to keep warm, and shift round now and then to give everyone a fair chance."

We huddled together like sheep and covered ourselves with our blankets. Occasionally we rose, stamped our feet and beat our hands, and then crouched down again.

When it was dark we put on our rackets and set out again. By daybreak we reached the landing-place. Rogers sent scouts to see if any of the enemy were out. They reported that there were two parties of them cutting wood on the east side of Lake Champlain.

French Woodcutters

Rogers now marched with fifty Rangers and as many Indians down to the isthmus, and we went up the same hill from which John Stark and Engineer Clark made their observations the year before. Everything looked different in the winter. We were acting as a guard to Mr. Bhreems, who went up to the crest of the hill and made sketches of the fort. Amos and I crept along the sidehill to where a few Indians and Rangers were watching some Frenchmen at work on the other side of the lake. They were cutting down trees and chopping them up into firewood.

"I suppose we've got to go over and capture some of those men, Amos."

"Yes; seems a p-pity, too, to attack men cutting wood. It puts me in mind of home. That's what I'd be doing now if I were there."

Rogers left a few scouts to watch these men, and the rest of us returned with the engineer.

The weather grew colder and colder. All this time we could have no fires. We watched each other to see if an ear or a nose were getting frost-bitten. I told Amos that his right ear looked pretty white, and that he had better see if there were any feeling in it.

He took off his mittens and pinched it.

"It don't hurt a bit. There isn't a mite of feeling."

I gave it a good rubbing, and he soon had feeling enough in it. "That comes from wearing such long ears, my boy."

His toes felt numb, and he went to a place that was bare of snow, took off his rackets, and stamped to get some life into his feet.

The regulars suffered much more than we did, for they had no rackets, and had been wallowing along in the deep snow. So many were frost-bitten that Rogers sent all the regulars back to Sabbath Day Point, and thirty Rangers with them.

Amos went with this party. They were told to build fires to keep themselves warm, and to wait for us.

They Capture Some Prisoners

At three in the morning the rest of us started out, Rogers, three lieutenants, one regular, and forty Rangers, and Captain Lotridge with forty-six Mohawk Indians.

We went southward to avoid being seen, and crossed South Bay about eight miles south of the fort. Here we came upon the trail of a large party of Indians who had gone toward Fort Edward; and Rogers sent off a couple of scouts to notify the men at the fort.

Then we turned and marched north in a couple of files, until we got within half a mile of the place where the French were cutting wood.

Two Rangers and two Indians were sent forward to scout. They returned and reported that about forty Frenchmen were at work opposite the fort.

"Now, boys," said Rogers, "get ready."

We threw down our blankets, and crept up silently until we were near them. Then we rushed on them and took several prisoners. Many others were killed by our Indians.

The French over at Fort Ticonderoga saw what was going on, and some eighty Canadians and Indians ran out of the fort followed by about one hundred and fifty regulars.

They pursued us.

"Spread out, boys, into a line abreast. Don't let them get a raking shot at you. Make for that rising ground over there."

"I thought the old man wouldn't clear out without giving them a little fun," said McKinstry. "'Twouldn't be neighborly after all the trouble they are taking to entertain us."

We retreated until we reached the rising ground, and then made a stand. The Canadians and Indians had snowshoes, and were a good deal ahead of the regulars. As they approached us, McKinstry said, "I wonder what kind of a shot you can make, Ben, with that French gun you've got. I'll take that big Frenchman over there with the blue shirt on."

"Well, then, I'll take the fellow next to him on the left."

They ran up toward us, and began to fire. We waited until they got close, and returned their fire. As the smoke blew away, McKinstry said,—

A Warm Reception

"Both of our men are down. You did well, Ben. It's a good deal easier to shoot a partridge than it is to shoot a man who is running at you with a gun in his hand."

The French fell back and waited for the regulars, and we started on again.

We reached a long ridge, and crossing to the further side of it, halted.

They came close to us, and McKinstry and I again chose our men. The Rangers poured a hot fire into them. We could not see until the smoke lifted.

"Your man is down, Ben; and I can see my man running away, but he limps."

"His toes may be frost-bitten, Mac."

"They weren't five minutes ago."

Our last fire completely routed the French, and they gave up the pursuit.

Two Rangers were killed; one of them was next to me as he fell. The regular who went with us was shot, and an Indian was wounded.

Of the enemy, some thirty were killed. We had the advantage in position, being sheltered by the ridge.

We kept on the go until twelve o'clock that night, having marched over fifty miles since we started in the morning. This, together with our three small scrimmages, might be considered an ample day's work. The snow was about four feet deep, and many of the party had their feet frozen, for it was bitter cold.

When we got to Sabbath Day Point, we found the rest of our men there, and a number of good fires. We warmed ourselves at them, and our companions brought us some warm food and drink.

Amos's ear was puffed up, and his toes were so sore he could hardly walk.

We were very tired, and rolled ourselves up in our blankets near the fires, and had a sound sleep.

The next day we marched as far as Long Island, and camped there that night.

At sunrise one of our Indians brought word that a large herd of deer was on the lake near the west side.

A Herd of Deer

McKinstry, Martin, Amos, and I got leave to go after them with some other Rangers and Indians. Amos started with us too.

"This is f-fun, Ben. A whole herd of d-deer waiting to be knocked over. Oh, my feet!"

He limped along, and the sweat stood out on his face. "It's no use, Ben. I can't do it. I call that t-tough luck—to be cheated out of the best chance for hunting I ever had. Goodbye."

He felt as bad over it as a boy of twelve would to lose Thanksgiving lunch.

We divided into two parties. A half a dozen Indians walked up the lake beyond the deer, so as to drive them toward us; and the rest of us went to the west side of the lake and up into the woods, until we were hidden from the lake.

We walked along on a path that was near the shore of the lake, until we were opposite the deer, and the Indians were already in a line on the further side of them.

"Now, boys," said McKinstry, "spread out, so that they can't run to the shore, and in this going we ought to get them all."

We went down on the ice and drove them toward the Indians and then formed a circle around them.

As we had rackets on, and the snow was deep, we could outrun the deer, and we killed the whole herd—twelve in all. Most of us shot our deer, but the Indians ran alongside of them and killed their deer with their hunting-knives.

"No more salt beef for us for a week or so," said McKinstry. "I've been longing for a bit of venison."

We cut up our deer, and making some rude sleds out of bark, placed our venison on them, and soon overtook the rest of our party, for they moved slowly.

Rogers had sent word to Fort Edward that many of the men were frost-bitten and unable to walk; and one hundred men with a number of Indian sleds were sent to us and met us on the lake. Amos got on one of these sleds, and we marched back to Fort Edward.

Chapter XV: Camp Discipline—Amherst's Angels—A Brush with the French, and the Loss of Captain Jacob

In the spring the provincial troops began to meet at Albany. Some of our officers had been recruiting during the winter, and they returned with their men.

John Stark had gone home in the fall to get married, and he brought back one hundred men whom he had enlisted at Amoskeag Falls. Two companies of Stockbridge Indians also joined us. There were fifty men in each of these companies.

By the first of June Amherst arrived at Fort Edward with part of the army, and Gage came up the river with the rest in boats. He brought the artillery and provisions with him.

The river was so high that the men could not use setting poles, and it took them two weeks to row up against the swift current.

Most of the provincial troops were without uniforms, and, as I have said, were ignorant of military life and discipline. Their officers wore a uniform of blue faced with scarlet, with metal buttons, and had laced waistcoats and hats. They were sober, sensible men.

When the provincials reached Fort Edward, they were drilled daily and taught to fire by platoon and to shoot at a mark. They were sent into the woods to learn how to fight.

One company from each regiment of the regulars was fitted out as light infantry and clothed lightly. Plenty of powder and ball was given to these men, and we used to go into the woods with them and give them an idea of wood fighting. We had a good deal of fun out of all this. It was solid comfort to go out with a batch of conceited fellows and show them how very green they were.

The soldiers were sent in bathing daily. The sick, if they had sufficient strength, had to go to the doctor for their medicines and to the river to wash and bathe. Amherst thought that spruce beer was a remedy against scurvy and made great quantities of it. We could have all we wanted at the rate of half a penny for a quart.

Military Punishments

Discipline was very rigid. Men were constantly being flogged. And one sometimes saw the drummers give a man two or three hundred stripes with the cat-o'-nine-tails, at the head of his regiment. Every now and then the drummers would rest, and a surgeon would examine the man to see if he could endure the remainder of the punishment. Some were punished by riding the wooden horse, and a couple were hanged for stealing cattle.

The woods along the path from Fort Edward were cut down for quite a distance on either side of the path, that the enemy might not ambush our parties. And little forts were built every three or four miles along the road. No one died of idleness that spring.

Our old uniforms were pretty well used up. When a jacket or a pair of breeches gave out, we replaced them with a deerskin shirt or breeches, which we made ourselves.

In the spring General Amherst gave the Rangers a new uniform. It was a blue cap or bonnet, such as the Highlanders wore, and a waistcoat and short jacket of black frieze lapelled with blue. There were no arms to the waistcoat or jacket, only armholes, and on the shoulders were little wings, such as the drummers and grenadiers wore. Hector called us Amherst's angels. The buttons were of white metal. We had drawers of linen or light canvas, and over them leggings of black frieze (*heavy wool fabric*) reaching to the thighs. From the calf down, they were buttoned with white metal buttons, and came over the feet like splatterdashes (*long leather leggings worn to protect stockings and trousers from spatters of mud while dashing about on horseback*). At our waist was fastened a short kilt of blue stuff, which reached nearly to the knees. Our dress was much like that of the Highlanders.

Most of the regulars who had joined us since the last campaign came from Louisburg, and had been sufficiently long in the land to lose a portion of that feeling of immense superiority which Englishmen have when fresh from the old country. Still they laughed heartily at the awkward appearance of the green provincial troops. And no one could help it who had experience in military life.

"Yankee Doodle"

"Ben," said Donald, "just listen to the green gawks singing and whistling that 'Yankee Doodle.' They think it is the finest tune on earth, and the latest martial music from England. I remember the bit of a surgeon who wrote that in fun two years ago, just to make sport of them."

"Well, Donald, I like it myself; and as our boys have taken it up, they're apt to fight well under it."

"'Deed, man, they'll no do anything with it. It's just a poor foolish tune."

How little we foresaw the popularity of that air. For years the bands of the British regiments played it in derision of the provincials. Percy's troops marched to Lexington to this music. They did not play it on their return. During the Revolution our men played it whenever the British were defeated, and the tune gradually became unpopular in the British army.

"Donald, our men may be green and awkward, but they are God-fearing men, most of them, members of the church; and they don't drink like fish, nor swear like pirates, as these newcomers do, whose conceit and overbearing ways are hard to endure."

"You're right there, Ben. It's no bad thing to have a gude opinion of oneself, provided it's not altogether too gude. And I maun say that these men put themselves too high. And a man should have a bridle on his tongue, and not be drinking too much of this nasty rum."

"They laugh at our ways of speaking, and say we speak through our noses. You of the Black Watch talk differently from them. I heard a captain, the other day, telling of pumpkins, which he called pompions. 'Yes,' he said, 'the pompion is a good vegetable, and an excellent succedaneum (*substitute*) to the cabbage, in the latter part of the winter.' What do you think of succedaneum, Donald?"

"'Deed, I think it's a fine word. I don't know what it means, but it has a grand sound. I'll manage to bring it in, in the future, when I hear people using big words. Benjamin, I'm obliged to you."

"A few days later, I heard this captain talking about the fogs in Nova Scotia, which he said, 'are owing to the steamy breath of fish and sea animals.' I put that down at once. If I could only hear him talk right along, I think I'd learn a good deal about nature. How do you like it?"

The Army Marches to Lake George

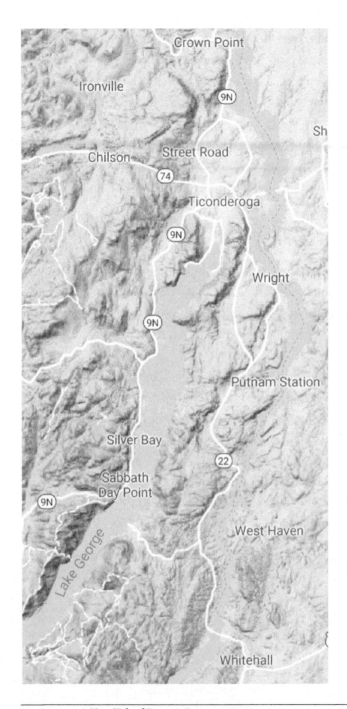

"He's a grand talker, Ben, and has an uncommon gude grip on the language. But I think his philosophy's gone to his head. He never lived among our Scotch mists, or he wouldn't be so befogged in his ideas."

When General Gage reached Fort Edward, he was sent over to Lake George with part of the army. Three companies of Rangers, under Captain Stark, went with him. The other three companies, under Rogers, remained behind.

On the 20th of June the rest of the army, under Amherst, marched to the lake.

Our three companies of Rangers, under Rogers, formed the advanced guard, and threw out flanking parties to scour the woods nearby. The artillery and baggage brought up the rear.

Then nearly a month was consumed in building boats and rafts to carry the artillery, in raising boats which had been sunk the previous fall, and in digging up cannon and stores that had been buried.

Amherst wished for information about the French, and Captain Jacob was sent on a scout to Lake Champlain. At the same time Rogers, McKinstry, Martin, and I set out to see what force the enemy had at Crown Point.

We put our birches into the water after dark. As I stepped into our birch, Jacob said, "Goodbye, Ben Comee! Never see you again. Heap Canawaugha Indians at Crown Point. Gray Wolf's friends. All want Ben Comee's scalp. Me heap sorry."

"Goodbye, Jacob. Take care you don't lose your own hair."

The Indians went along the south shore, and we struck across for the other side. The enemy had several batteaux on the lake, and we paddled quietly in the dark until we reached the other shore. As it became light, we lifted our canoe from the water, and hid it in the bushes.

Rogers started off through the woods, and we followed him in a file. We climbed a mountain near Ticonderoga and had a good view of the fort. We stayed there for a couple of hours, counting the different bodies of soldiers. There seemed to be about three thousand men in the garrison,—regulars, Canadians, and Indians. Then we came down and went north to Crown Point. We ascended a hill, and looked down on the fort. It was deserted. The French had concentrated all their men at Ticonderoga.

Captain Jacob in Hot Water

McKinstry called out: "Look up the lake. Captain Jacob is in hot water. Those two birches (*canoe*) that are being chased are his, certain."

"Yes; he and his men are in those two, and there are seven birches after them. About thirty men. It's a pretty slim chance he's got. Now they're firing."

Both parties were shooting at each other. As they neared the shore, we lost sight of them behind a point, but could still hear them popping away.

Rogers said, "Captain Jacob is in a fix. Presence of mind is a good thing, but absence of body is a great deal better in a case like this, and we'd better light out of here at once, and get out of the way before they run across our trail. There's too few of us to help him. We must look out for our own scalps. Hurry up."

We went back into the woods a long distance before we turned south to go to Lake George. We reached camp the next evening, and on the following day a wounded Indian came in and said that Captain Jacob and the other four Indians were captured.

There was a report that he was sent to Montreal, but it is more likely that he was tortured and sang his death song at the stake.

At last the rafts were ready for the artillery, and on the 21st day of July the army embarked and moved down the lake in four columns. The Rangers headed the column on the right. To the left of us was a column of two brigades of regulars. The third column was mainly made up of boats and rafts carrying the artillery and provisions, and the provincials formed the fourth column.

The Army Embarks

A raft called the *Invincible Radeau*, which carried nine twelve-pounders, led the army, and the *Halifax* sloop brought up the rear.

From these, signals were displayed which informed us what to do. The weather was hazy. There was a strong wind which made quite a sea, and put the artillery in considerable danger. Whenever the wind was favorable, we spread our blankets for sails, which helped us very much. There were in all about eleven thousand men,—regulars and provincials.

Chapter XVI: The Rangers to the Front—Captain Stark's Tale of Capture—To Attack the St. Francis Indians

We reached the outlet at night, and remained in the boats, tossed about on the water, which was quite rough. The Rangers were the first to land. We marched by the portage path to the sawmills, and crossed the bridge to the rising ground on the further side.

A party of the enemy met us there, but we killed some of them, drove them off, and took several prisoners. Soon after, the grenadiers and light infantry came up, and were followed by the rest of the army, which remained overnight at the sawmills. The Canadians and Indians crept up again, and fired on us from the bushes.

"S-Some of your Canawaugha friends, B-Ben, come to pay you a call."

Rangers Advance to Lake Champlain

We got behind trees and bushes, and we and the French picked each other off until night came.

Several of our men were wounded. How much the enemy suffered I do not know, as the Indians drag off their dead. This would seem to be a matter of no consequence, but I can assure you, that after you have been four or five hours behind a tree, and heard the bullets plug into it, or zip through the grass and bushes, close by, it's a great downfall when the enemy have been driven off, to search the ground in front of you, and find no dead or wounded, when you could take your oath that you had hit three or four.

On the 23rd, the Rangers were sent across the plain, to take a position on the cleared land, next to Lake Champlain, near the breastwork.

When we got there, we found ourselves close to a small entrenchment, and the men in it opened fire on us.

"There's no sense, Ben, in standing here, to be shot at," said Martin.

"No; let's drive them out of that entrenchment, and get behind it ourselves. Come on, boys."

We ran toward this earthwork, firing as we advanced, and the French cleared out as we were climbing over the bank.

The army now came over to the lake, and the artillery was brought up by the provincials. Although the breastworks had been greatly strengthened, the enemy abandoned them, and withdrew to the fort. The breastworks afforded a good shelter for our men.

Our army began to throw up earthworks, and at night the Rangers were sent into the trenches to pick off the enemy, and distract their attention from the workmen.

All of our cannon had now been brought over; and on the night of the 24th Bourlemaque, the French commander, abandoned the fort with most of his army, and rowed down the lake, leaving four hundred men to defend the place.

As soon as our guns were in place, a sharp cannonade began from both sides.

Amherst wished to know what the soldiers under Bourlemaque were doing, and a number of Rangers had been sent down the lake to watch them, and some of them were constantly returning with news of the movements of the enemy.

The French Abandon Ticonderoga

A batteau and two whaleboats had been brought over from Lake George; and on the night of the 25th Rogers ordered sixty of the Rangers to embark in these boats, to cut a boom which the French had placed across the lake, just above the fort.

When we were halfway to the boom, we saw lights moving at the fort, and the enemy ran down to the shore, and began to get into their boats.

Rogers cried out: "They're getting ready to leave. Go for them, boys!"

Our boats attacked some of the enemy's batteaux which were separated from the main body. We rowed among them and fired right and left. One of the crews showed fight, but we killed three or four of them, and the rest jumped overboard and swam ashore. Rogers sent our boat after another boat. I was in the bow, and kept firing at them, until at last they turned to the shore, and escaped into the woods. At about ten o'clock, while we were still fighting, the fort blew up with a tremendous noise.

We remained at this place, and in the morning took possession of the boats that we had driven ashore. They contained a large quantity of baggage,—fifty kegs of powder, and a number of cannon ball. Later in the day I examined the fort. It was completely destroyed by the explosion of its powder magazine.

Two hundred Rangers, under Captain Brewer, were sent to watch the enemy at Crown Point. The rest of us were sent to the sawmills, to look out for flying parties of the enemy. We remained there two weeks.

On the 12th of August we were ordered to the front of the army, and the whole army marched to the fort at Crown Point, which had been blown up and destroyed by the enemy.

I had not had a chance to talk to Captain Stark for a long time, and when we camped at Crown Point, I went over to his quarters. He took me into his hut and gave me a pipe.

A Foolish Errand

"I'm glad to see you, Comee. It's been some time since we met, and I shall not see you again this campaign. I received orders today to take two hundred men and cut a path through the woods to Fort No. 4. I am very glad of it, for it will take me out of a fix I should have been in, if I had remained here."

"How's that, Captain John?"

"General Amherst has sent Captain Kennedy and some other officers to try and gain over the St. Francis Indians. I think it is a foolish errand, which will breed trouble. I don't want to fight them. That is, I don't mind fighting them, if they come down here, spoiling for a row. But I don't want to go and attack them in their own region, for I am a member of that tribe: I was adopted by them. You never suspected that I was a full-fledged Indian warrior, did you, Ben?"

"No, indeed. How in the world can that be?"

"When I grew up, I went trapping and hunting at Baker's River, in the spring of 1752, with David Stinson, Amos Eastman, and my brother William. We made a camp with bark and boughs. There was plenty of game, and we trapped over £500 worth of furs before the first of April. On the 27th day of that month we saw the tracks of Indians, and decided to get out of that region at once. I was twenty-three years old, the youngest of our party, and was sent to take up the traps."

"Seems to me, Captain John, if I had £500 of furs, and saw tracks of Indians, I'd have lit out with my furs, and not waited to pick up traps."

"That would have been the right thing to do. That's what a sensible man would have done. But if you had been there, you'd probably have been just as big a fool as we were. You see if we had come back without our traps, someone in the settlements would have been sure to laugh at the scare we had over nothing. And we were young idiots, and took the risk.

"Just about sunset, I was stooping over the water, taking up a trap, when I heard a sound like 'O whish!' I looked up, and saw several redskins pointing their guns at me.

The Captives

"They asked me where our camp was, and I led them two miles away from it up the river.

"As I did not return to camp, the boys began to fire their guns to call me back. The Indians ran through the woods, and got below them on the river in order to head off the canoe as it came down.

"Eastman was on shore, and Stinson and my brother William were in the canoe. Just after daybreak they caught Eastman as he was walking along the bank. The Indians told me to hail the others, and call them to the shore. I shouted to them: 'The Indians have got Eastman and me. Go down the further shore.' They paddled away, and the Indians rose and fired. I knocked up the muzzles of the guns of those near me, and as the rest fired, I hit all the guns I could. One shot killed Stinson, and a bullet went through the paddle which my brother held.

"I cried out, 'They've all fired, Bill. Get away as quick as you can.' He paddled off, and the Indians gave me a good pounding, for which I could not blame them."

"They must have been pretty angry with you."

"They were just boiling over, and at the same time they kind of liked me for it, too.

"They were St. Francis Indians. There were ten of them under their chief, Francis Titigaw. They took us up to the Connecticut River, where we were joined by two Indians who had been left there. Then we went to the upper Coos Intervale. Three of the Indians were sent with Eastman to the village of St. Francis. The rest of us hunted on a small creek. They let me do a little trapping, and gave me the skins of a couple of beavers that I killed.

"Early in June we arrived at St. Francis, and they made Eastman and me run the gauntlet. The young Indians formed two lines, and we were to run down between them. Each Indian had a club or stick, and they gave Eastman and me two poles about eight feet long, with the skin of an animal or bird tied to the end.

"They taught us some words to sing as we passed down the line, and pretty sassy words they were. Eastman sang, 'I'll beat all your young men.' This made the young braves angry and every one struck at him, so that he was pretty well used up when he got through the lines.

Running the Gauntlet

"When my turn came, I sang, 'I'll kiss all your young women.' I had a good, strong pole, and made up my mind that I would not be the only one who got the blows. As I ran through the lines, I whacked away, right and left, and this surprised them so much that I got through with but little harm. Perhaps you think, as others do, that there is no fun in an Indian. But the old men who sat nearby were immensely tickled as their young men went down, and they showed their pleasure.

"The first man who struck me was a young fellow eighteen or nineteen years old. I knocked him down, and he felt so small about it that I did not see him again while I was with them.

"An Indian doesn't work. He makes his squaws and prisoners do that. They set me at work with the squaws, hoeing corn. I hoed up the corn instead of the weeds. They tried to make me hoe the right way. But I made up my mind that if they wouldn't hoe corn, I wouldn't. I threw my hoe into the river, and told them that I was a warrior and not a squaw to hoe corn.

"Instead of being angry with me, they liked me for this, and the old chief adopted me.

"They called me the young chief and treated me well. I learned something of their language and ways of fighting that has been of advantage to me. I never saw any prisoner of war treated with so much kindness as I was by those St. Francis Indians. After I had been at the village five weeks, Mr. Wheelwright, of Boston, and Captain Stevens, of No. 4, came to Montreal, to redeem some Massachusetts prisoners. But not finding them, they bought Eastman and me, and we returned with them by the way of Albany. I worked hard afterward, and paid off my debt to the Massachusetts Province. If there is to be any fight with these Indians, I shall be glad if I am at work cutting out a road to Fort No. 4."

Early in September we heard that Captain Kennedy, who had been sent to these St. Francis Indians, to persuade them to abandon the French and make peace with us, had been made a prisoner by them with the men who accompanied him, and had been sent to Montreal.

Captain Kennedy Made Prisoner

General Amherst was very angry at their treachery. On the afternoon of September 13 we received orders to be in readiness to explore the country west of us. We were told that we should go a short distance in boats and then strike out to the west.

"This seems a silly trip, Ben," said Martin. "Fooling about in the woods where there is no enemy. Our army ought to be following the French, driving them down to the St. Lawrence. Then we could join our forces with Wolfe's, and finish up the war."

"Sergeant Munro tells me that Amherst thinks he should restore the fort and build some boats and ships first."

"Maybe, maybe; I'm not a general, but I believe that when you've got the enemy on the run, you ought to keep them on the run until they give in, and not sit down and give them a chance to get strong again."

That night we embarked in whaleboats. There were about two hundred men in our party. It was made up of a few of Gage's light infantry, under Captain Dunbar, and the rest were Rangers, among whom were fifty Mohegan Indians from Stockbridge. We rowed over to the east shore and went down the lake. Several canoes were sent ahead to warn us if any of the enemy were out. Cloth was wound round our oars where they rested in the rowlocks. We had orders not to utter a word, to make no noise.

The boats moved in single file close to the shore where it was darkest. Before daybreak we landed and lifted the boats from the water and carried them into the woods. We lay hidden there during the day. We did not believe that we were going to the west, but could not guess the purpose of the expedition.

The next night we embarked again, and rowed slowly in perfect silence with an advanced guard of canoes.

Night after night we did this, always keeping in the shadow of the shore; and as we got toward the lower part of the lake, we did not start until late at night, and pulled our boats up into the bushes long before the day began to break. Several times our scouts came back and whispered that the enemy's boats were out. Then we went in close to the shore and waited until they were out of hearing distance.

A Mysterious Expedition

We were not allowed to make fires, and as we approached the lower end of the lake and lay hidden in the woods, we could see sloops and boats of the enemy out on the lake in the daytime. We had to proceed slowly and with the utmost caution.

If we had not been on a perilous expedition into the enemy's country to some unknown point and for some mysterious purpose, about which we were worrying, this trip down the lake would have been delightful. The leaves were just changing color. The days were perfect. The lake was beautiful, and we should have gazed with pleasure at the boats that we saw, had we not known that they were full of enemies who would have been well pleased to take our scalps and roast us at the stake.

On the fifth day out, by some accident there was an explosion of gunpowder, and several of the men were burned and had to be sent back. Some were sick, and returned with them, so that by the time we reached Missisquoi Bay at the lower end of the lake our force was reduced to one hundred and forty-five men.

It was apparent that this was no expedition to the west, and we were astonished as we advanced night after night into the enemy's country and close to their camp.

Edmund knew where we were going, but he was as close-mouthed as an oyster.

"What in the w-world are we up to? Are we going to attack the French army with one hundred and fifty men? I don't like these expeditions of Major Rogers. I wish we had a good safe commander like that c-colonel who was sent out on the lake to stop a party of French and Indians, and landed on an island and formed his men in a circle round him, and p-p-prayed that the Lord would send us a long war and a b-b-bloodless war, and kept on praying until the enemy went by. A fellow has some chance to keep his hair on his head with a g-good c-careful commander like that; but this Rogers don't care where he g-goes or how many get k-killed, so long as he can do something startling. What in time are we up to?"

Amos Prefers a Careful Commander

I had been thinking over my talk with Captain Stark, and said,—

"I know what Rogers is about to do. We are going right up into Canada to the St. Lawrence River, to attack the St. Francis Indians who made Captain Kennedy and his men prisoners."

As I said this, Edmund laughed, and I knew that I had hit it.

"By the g-great Horn Spoon! That b-beats anything that Weaver David ever dreamed of. Is that it, Edmund?"

"I can't tell you where we are going, but don't say a word of what you suspect; for if any of our party were caught and knew where we were going, it would be sure death for the rest of us; so just hold your mouth and don't talk."

Chapter XVII: March to the Village—The Retreat

We landed at Missisquoi Bay and pulled our boats up into the woods. Near them we hid the provisions for our return. We distributed the rest of the food among us, put it on our backs in sacks, and started off to the northeast.

We left behind us a couple of Stockbridge Indians to watch the boats and give us notice if they were discovered. We had only marched two days when these two Indians caught up with us.

"Frenchmen and Indians find boats. Heap big party follow us. Three hundred men."

Rogers said, "Boys, we are out to punish some Indians, and the only course for us is to outmarch the enemy, do our work, and get out of the way."

We plodded along day after day, from daybreak to dark, most of the time through spruce bogs where the water was sometimes ankle-deep, and at times up to our thighs. We were wet all the time, and our shoes began to rot and go to pieces.

Damp Walking

At night we cut down trees, laid boughs from one tree to another, and slept on them to keep out of the water. Nine days we marched and slept in this manner. It was a terrible strain even to hardy men such as we were, accustomed to forest life.

Amos said, "We're just like a procession of cold, miserable frogs, h-hopping along through the water. This is the biggest fool trip I ever heard of."

"Think of the glory, Amos, of going into the heart of the enemy's country and punishing these Indians."

"Glory be h-hanged! I wish I was with Davy, hunting foxes and listening to his big stories of what he did do, or would have done if something hadn't happened."

"But when you get back, Amos, you can crush him by telling of this trip."

"Yes, when I g-get back. When I get back! I should rather be b-back without the story. L-Looks to me as if Davy's chance of hearing it is rather slim."

On the tenth day after we left Missisquoi Bay we reached a river.

Rogers said, "Boys, this is the St. Francis River. You have of course guessed by this time that we are going to punish the St. Francis Indians for making Captain Kennedy and his companions prisoners when they went to them with a flag of truce. I did not tell you before, because it was not safe to do so. If any of you had been waylaid, it was better he should not know where the party was going, for the Indians would torture him to make him tell all he knew, and then the French and Indians would be warned. Now they can only guess where we are to strike. The village of St. Francis is on the St. Lawrence River, at the mouth of this river, and on the further side. It is some fifteen miles from here. We shall attack them in the night. You need have no feelings of pity for them or mercy. They are the tribe who have been harassing our frontier for the past ninety years. I know that they have killed four or five hundred good New England men, beside the women and children they have slain and carried off. This river has a swift current, and we must put our packs on our shoulders and join arms, with the tallest and strongest up the river, so as to help each other. Come, Martin, and you, Comee, let's see how you can keep your legs today."

Crossing the River

Rogers put me near the head of the line, as I was considered a strong man. We went into the water with arms locked, and struggled against the current. Though the river was over four feet deep, we got across with few accidents.

Several men were swept off their feet, and some guns were lost, but we arrived safely at the further shore.

We made a small raft, put our powder-horns on it, and pulled it to and fro across the stream until all were carried over.

Scouts were sent ahead, and flanking parties were thrown out. We advanced cautiously in three files. I did not like this kind of an expedition, and said so to Martin, who was next to me.

"I can't bear this sneaking up on the Indians, and jumping on them in the dead of night when they are sound asleep. I like a good square fight of give and take."

"Don't be a fool, Ben. Those Indians have killed and scalped two of your family. If you had lived on the frontier all your life as I have, you would be glad to pay them back in their own coin, eye for eye, tooth for tooth, scalp for scalp. I have had so many friends killed by them, good quiet people, who never harmed any one. Almost every year, and sometimes several times a year, I have gone with others to help drive these devils away from some fort or town. And the sights that I have seen make me hate the redskins worse than poison. And, Ben, you know enough of them yourself. How many Rangers have been tormented by them and scalped? Remember John McKeen! How he was stripped and tied to a tree; then the red devils danced around him, howled at him, taunted him, and threw their knives at him until he was full of holes from head to foot. Have you forgotten what they did then? Put a pine splinter in every wound he had, set them on fire and made a living torch of him."

McKinstry's Score

"Yes, Martin, one does not forget such things, nor how they tortured others, and then made them run the gauntlet, hacked at them with knives and tomahawks until they fell, and then scalped them. They deserve to be killed like snakes, but I don't like to do it. No matter how mean or treacherous my enemy, I want a good stand-up fair fight. I am a soldier. I am under orders, and I shall do the work; but I hate it."

"You needn't be squeamish, Ben. They are double our number, and if we don't kill them by a surprise, they will kill us."

McKinstry had been listening, and said, "It's plain, Ben, that you have never lived where there were Injuns. Your injuries are too far off. They don't touch you. I have a score to pay that I have been wiping off for the past thirty years. Here's my tally-stick. Look at the notches."

He pulled at a string that was round his neck, and showed me a little stick with seventeen notches in it.

"I have killed that number of Indians. Every notch I have added made my heart feel lighter. Every chance I have to kill a St. Francis Indian, awake or asleep, makes me happy. I want to see the whole tribe wiped off the earth."

The land on this side of the river was higher than the region through which we had been travelling, and we were not so much troubled by mosquitoes, which had nearly driven us crazy in the swamps.

The clear, crisp air dried our clothes before nightfall, and we slept sound, breathing in the clean smell of the fir balsams.

On the next day, the 22nd, after we left Crown Point, we made a cautious advance. Rogers halted us and climbed a tree. He said that he could see the village about three miles off.

Rogers went ahead with Lieutenant Turner and Ensign Avery to inspect the village, and we lay down and waited. The moon was about three-quarters full. He returned at two in the morning, and said,—

"We crawled up close to their village. The Indians are having a great frolic. They have a keg of rum and are drinking it, and are dancing round the fires. I think there must be a wedding going on. They will sleep sound."

They Attack the Village

At three o'clock we crept up to within five hundred yards of the village, and laid aside our packs and prepared for the fight. We had one hundred and forty-two men, all told.

We lay concealed in the forest until the Indians were asleep. Rogers divided us into three parties, and about an hour before daylight ordered us to attack the village on three sides. The St. Lawrence River was on the fourth side. We rushed into the village, through its lanes, kicking the yelping dogs aside, and stationed ourselves before the huts. Above the doors were poles, from which dangled rows of scalps, as if they were garlands of flowers.

I stood by the door of a hut, and as an Indian came out I shot him; and when the next appeared, with a dazed, frightened look on his face, I brained him with the butt of my gun, and then pulled out my hatchet and chopped away at them as they ran by. Martin, Edmund, and Amos were near me. Sometimes several Indians made a rush, and we closed up and fought them.

It was cruel, bloody butchery. But the sight of the poles with the scalps of English men, women, and children hanging from them made us mad with rage, and we killed the Indians like rats as they dashed out of their huts. Some reached the canoes, but were followed and cut down. Few escaped. Some squaws were killed too. We were all mixed up. It was impossible to spare them. They fought like wildcats with knives and hatchets, and we had to kill them or be killed ourselves.

By sunrise the bloody work was over. Almost all the Indians had been slain. As we looked round and saw nearly six hundred English scalps dangling in front of the huts, we felt no sorrow for what we had done.

Still, it was a grim, dreadful piece of work. The dead Indians lay around in the lanes between the huts, in some places in heaps, stiffening in death, smeared with blood, and the Stockbridge Indians were already at work scalping them.

A Grim Piece of Work

We ourselves were covered with blood, and looked like butchers from the shambles. It was not all Indian blood. They were not lambs, and gave us many a wound before we got the better of them. Edmund and Amos came to me.

"How did you get through it, Ben?"

"All right, but a few cuts. I hope I don't look as villainous as you or Amos."

"I d-don't know how I look. B-But if I saw you or Edmund round my place looking as you d-do now, I'd shoot you at sight."

Rogers ordered us to set fire to all the houses except those which were storehouses for corn. One house was a mass-house with pictures hanging up inside. We found some silver cups and plates in it, and a silver image some ten inches high. In the other houses we found many things which they had carried off from the settlements.

Most of the Rangers had lost relatives and friends in these Indian fights, and were examining the scalps carefully. McKinstry was looking them over with an intense, eager air. Seeing me, he said, "It's a foolish search. Thirty years have passed since they killed my sweetheart and ruined my life. I was looking for a lock of hair like this."

He pulled a little pouch from his breast, opened it, and unfolding some fine cloth, showed me a lock of golden hair.

"The Indians surprised the garrison house where she lived and killed all but her. We got word of it soon. We started out with a large party and pursued them. We followed them day and night, and as they were being overtaken they killed and scalped her. I found her dead body on the ground, and from that day to this I have sought revenge. Last night was the happiest I have had for years. The tribe that killed her is wiped out, and I killed six of them myself."

Rogers had been questioning some of the prisoners. He turned to us and said,—

"Hurry up, boys; we must get out of this place quick. There's no time to go back after our packs. There's a party of three hundred French and Indians four miles below, on the St. Lawrence, looking for us, and two hundred Frenchmen and sixteen Indians went to Wigwam Martinac a few days ago, expecting we would attack that place. They will all be after us soon. Load yourselves up with corn from the corn houses. Take all you can, for we shall have little else to live upon, as the game is scanty in the country through which we shall pass."

The Village in Flames

We put the corn in our pockets and in any sacks that we could find, placed them on our backs, and left the village a mass of flames.

"We must strike through the woods to the head waters of the Connecticut River, and follow it down to Fort No. 4. We can't go back by the way we came, for the French and Indians could easily collect a force that would overpower us. I sent word to Amherst to have plenty of provisions for us at the mouth of the Ammonusuc River, and we can get there all right."

We released all our prisoners but a couple of boys, and started off, taking with us six Englishmen whom we found in captivity. Edmund said,—

"I'm glad to leave this place. It's too much like a slaughter-house. Orders are orders, and we have to execute them. But faith! I can't see but that we have been doing just what these Indians have done for the last ninety years."

"The work had to be done, and we did it. I can't say I feel proud of it either. I wonder how we are going to get out of this scrape."

"At the l-little end of the h-horn. It seems that we shall starve in the region th-through which we shall travel; and we should all be killed if we w-went in any other direction; and I guess these Indians will follow us p-pretty sharp, whichever way we go."

We marched in a body to the southeast at the top of our speed. At night we stopped, parched our corn and ate it. In the morning at daybreak we started on again.

In eight days we reached Lake Memphremagog. The corn was giving out, and Rogers separated us into small parties, each with a guide who had been up the Connecticut River. He told the different parties to keep away from one another, that they might the more readily find sufficient game to support them, and to meet at the Coos Intervale land at the mouth of the Ammonusuc River. That was the place to which he had requested Amherst to send the supplies.

The Ambush

Our Mohegan Indians left us, and went south toward their home, for they thought the hunting would be better in that direction and the risk no greater. They reached home without losing a man.

Edmund, McKinstry, Amos, and I were with Rogers's party. The Indians pursued us closely. We came to a narrow valley, and Rogers said,—

"We'll try an ambush on them, and see how they like it. After you enter the valley, get up into the woods on either side. Don't fire until they are well in the valley."

The rear portion of our party were exchanging shots with the Indians, dodging from tree to tree. They came down the valley followed by the redskins. When they were well in the trap, we opened fire on the Indians and killed a number. They began to run back. We reloaded hastily, and, after pouring a second volley into them, rushed on them. McKinstry knocked an Indian down, but was shot by another, whom I killed with my hatchet. I turned to McKinstry. He lay on the ground gasping for breath, shot through the body.

"It's all up with me, Ben."

I tried to staunch the blood.

"It's no use; I feel I'm dying. I always liked you, Ben. May your life be happy. Goodbye."

He closed his eyes, and his breast heaved hard as he drew short, quick breaths. Presently he opened his eyes again. He did not notice me, but seemed to see something above him. A smile came over his face, and he said,—

"Yes, Mary, I'm coming, dear."

Then his breathing ceased. We buried him in the valley, levelled the grave, threw wood on it, and burnt the brush around that the ashes might conceal the spot where he was laid. Then we hurried on again.

Three days later two of Ensign Avery's men joined us, and reported that some of them had been captured by the Indians, and that several had been tortured and burnt at the stake. These two had escaped in the night, while the Indians were dancing round their companions. The next day the few who were left of Avery's party met us.

A Choice Morsel

We marched along, keeping a sharp lookout for squirrels, chipmunks, or any kind of animal that might serve as food. Thus we travelled over rocky mountains and through wet swamps, pursued by Indians, faint from hunger, worn out with fatigue and exposure, hardly able to walk. We had no blankets or shelter. The nights were cold and frosty, and when it rained we were soaked and chilled to the bone.

We found almost no game. Edmund had the luck to shoot a big white owl. We plucked it, cut it up, and drew lots for the different portions. I got a leg. It was tough—almost as tough as our fate. But after one has been chewing leather straps for sustenance, an old owl's leg tastes good. I would not have sold it for its weight in the most precious stones.

I shall not tell all the horrors of that march,—the pangs of hunger that we suffered, the greed for food, the sights that I saw, nor what men did in their despair. Some things had better remain unwritten.

Chapter XVIII: Starvation—Drifting Down the Ammonusuc—Fort No. 4, and Good Fortune at Last

At last we arrived at the Ammonusuc River, where our provisions were to meet us, and found *nothing*.

Fires were still burning which showed us that the relief party had been there, and had left just before we arrived. We shouted and fired our guns, but got no response. We learned afterward that the lieutenant who had brought the supplies had waited two days for us, and then quitted the place two hours before we arrived, taking the provisions with him. He heard our guns, but thought that they were fired by Indians, and kept on his way down the river.

Our condition was terrible. We had been stumbling along, feeble, gaunt, half crazed by hunger and fatigue. But the expectation of food, the certainty that we should find plenty at the Ammonusuc, had nerved us up to the effort to reach it, and now it was gone. It had been there and was gone. We broke down completely and cried and raved. Some became insane.

I have already said that I did not like Rogers for several good reasons. But he was a man of tremendous nerve, energy, and resource. Though his great strength had been wasted by starvation, so that he could hardly walk, he still remained the leader, and said,—

"Don't lose your courage, men. I'll save all of you. It is sixty miles from here to Fort No. 4. Bring some dry logs. Hurry up. I am going to make a raft, and float down to No. 4 and fetch back food and help."

We brought logs and made a raft.

"You can find enough lily-roots and ground-nuts to keep you alive until I return. If any of you do not know how to clean and cook them, Captain Grant will show you. I promise you I will have all the food you want at this place in ten days."

Starvation

He got on the raft with Captain Ogden, an Indian boy and Martin, who had been over the river before. They poled and paddled it to the middle of the river, and drifted down the stream out of sight.

The next day two more men crept into camp and reported that the Indians had attacked their party several days before, and had killed Lieutenant Turner of the Rangers, Lieutenant Dunbar of Gage's light infantry, and that of all their party they alone had escaped.

It was horrible to see the wild, haggard men stagger in, and to witness their despair when they received nothing to eat but such lily-roots and ground-nuts as we could find and boil. There was but little nourishment in them.

Ben Bradley left camp with three companions. They put on their packs. Ben looked at his compass, and said,—

"Goodbye, boys. In three days we shall be at home."

They were never afterward seen alive. Several years later some hunters from the Merrimac found a skeleton in the White Mountains. They knew it was Bradley's from the hair, and the peculiar leather strap with which his cue was tied.

After Rogers had been gone three days, I said to Edmund:—

"I can't stand this any longer. This place is like a mad-house. We shall go crazy if we stay here. Let us get some logs, make a raft, and drift down the river."

We talked it over that afternoon, and the next morning began building a raft. It was a rickety little affair. We finished it in one day, but were so feeble that we found it hard work. We cut a couple of saplings for poles, and took some wood, from which we whittled a couple of paddles.

One of the men, who had been over the river before, said,—

"Look out for a waterfall and rapids, some twenty miles down, boys. Don't get carried over them, or you'll be lost. And there's another bad fall and rapids below that."

We poled the raft into the current, and let it drift. Toward night we paddled to the shore and camped there.

The Raft is Lost

In the morning we shot a squirrel, and during the day got another. Toward evening we heard the sound of the falls, and poled to the shore. The night was cold. We had no shelter. It rained heavily. We were drenched and almost frozen. In the morning our little strength was gone. We got on our raft, and poled it along until we were close to the falls; and then put in to the shore. Amos held the raft, while Edmund and I went below, in the hope that it might not be badly broken, as it came over, and that we could save it. We waded into the cold water, and Amos let the raft go. It was dashed on the rocks, as it passed over the falls, and was completely broken up. The logs drifted out of our reach. Thoroughly chilled, exhausted, and discouraged, we climbed the bank. We saw that fires had been made and trees burnt down, and then burnt into lengths.

"This is some of Rogers's work," said Edmund.

"He must have lost his raft as we did, and burned the trees to get logs of the right lengths to make a new raft."

"I hope he didn't spend much time over it. For I can't go any further, and B-Ben is all of a shake, and looks mighty poor."

"I guess last night did for me, Amos. I've got some kind of fever coming on. Start a fire if you can, and let us try to warm ourselves."

The ground was wet, but Amos and Edmund collected an armful of dry wood from sheltered spots. We rubbed some gunpowder into a rag, and sprinkled more over it. We held it near the lock of the gun, and flashed some powder in the pan. This lighted the rag, and we covered it with fine shavings which we had whittled, and made a fire.

"A canoe from below ought to reach here by tomorrow. I can keep up until then."

"Hush! I heard a p-partridge, and I've g-got strength enough to go after him." The tough, wiry fellow took his gun, and went into the woods.

Welcome Visitors

We heard a bang, and he came out with a partridge, which we roasted and divided among us. It only served to sharpen our hunger.

"There must be more of these p-partridges in there. I'm g-going to try again. I feel b-better."

"I will go too," said Edmund.

They walked into the woods, and in half an hour I heard a couple of shots, and they came out with two birds. We roasted them, ate them, and felt that we were saved. We kept a good fire going, built a rough shelter of boughs, and slept quite comfortably that night, though the fever troubled me somewhat. The next morning we made an attempt to find more birds, but were unsuccessful. A little after noon we saw a birch coming up the stream with three men in it. They waved their hands to us, and landed where we were at the foot of the falls. They shook hands, and one of them said,—

"You look pretty peaked, boys. I guess a little food and drink won't hurt you."

We ate greedily, and the food put warmth and life into us. We asked about Rogers.

"He's at No. 4. His raft was swept over these falls, and he and his men had a narrow escape. Then he made a new raft and was nearly lost at the falls below. We'd like to stop longer with you, boys, but can't. We're carrying food to the fellows up the river."

"You must get there as quick as you can. We left about seventy men up there, starving and going mad for want of food."

"Some more birches are to follow us in a couple of days, and you'll meet them on your way down."

They gave us some food and then made the carry, up by the falls, and left us. We ate and drank some more, and then slept for an hour. When we woke up, we felt much stronger, and went to work making another raft. The next day we completed the raft early in the morning; and drifted down to the waterfall of which they had spoken. We kept our ears and eyes open, and went ashore in time to avoid it. We had built a fire and were making a shelter, when three more canoes came up, and we camped together with the men. We had all that we could eat and it was delightful to us to meet these clean, healthy, robust men, full of life.

Fort No. 4

In the morning they helped us lower our raft down the fifty feet of rapids. They gave us some nails, and we added to our raft and made it stronger, and then poled it out into the river, and drifted down with the current. We arrived at Fort No. 4 at sunset. It was the 9th of November. We had spent two months in that dreadful, barren wilderness. When we came in sight of the fort, and poled our raft to the shore, men and women in good Christian dress came running down to meet us. Our hearts rose up in our throats. We could not speak from our happiness. The tears rolled down our cheeks and we sobbed from joy.

How fine they looked, those men with their clean-shaven faces, and their hair neatly done up in cues! And how beautiful and kind the women!

Such few clothes as we still had were in rags. Our hair and beards were long and matted together; our faces and hands black from exposure and dirt and grime. We felt ashamed of our appearance and would gladly have sneaked in unseen. But they made of us as if we had been three prodigal sons. And the flesh-pots, the fatted calf, and the honey were all offered to us.

Rogers claimed us for a short time, to get news from the camp, and told us he was going up the next morning.

We had a supper of the best there was in the fort, and you can guess how it looked and tasted to men who had lived for weeks on corn and leather straps and nothing; and who had watched with greedy eyes the cutting up of an old white owl.

They gave us a room, with soap and tubs of warm water, and we got rid of some of the grime, cut off our beards, shaved our faces, and put on the clothes they left for us. Amos said,—

"B-Ben, I feel as if No. 4 must be p-pretty near h-heaven."

"Yes! But it isn't up the river."

When we came out, the men crowded round to hear our adventures. Amos started to tell the story, and when he got hung up on a word, Edmund would go on with the tale.

Ben Has a Fever

I felt hot and feeble and sick. My head ached. I became dizzy, and finally asked someone to take me to a room where I could lie down, and I went to bed. I haven't any clear idea of what happened afterward. I have a faint recollection of Edmund and Amos bending over me, saying Goodbye. But I do remember that Indian who tried again and again to scalp me. John Stark drove him off several times, but he kept coming back, and at last caught me by the hair, ran his knife round my head, braced his foot on my shoulder, pulled, and I felt my scalp go. Then I knew nothing more until I opened my eyes, and saw the rafters above, and the bedclothes about me.

I smelt smoke, and heard the wood snap and crackle. Beside the fireplace a girl was seated, knitting. Such a pretty girl, the loveliest I had ever seen. I watched her knit, and then stop and count the stitches. How beautiful she was, with her light brown hair, the pretty side face, with the fresh color in it! Her figure was lithe, supple, full of grace. I thought at once of Shakespeare's Rosalind. My heart went out to her. As I gazed, she looked up, and turned a pair of big brown eyes at me. I had never been in love before. But, as she rose and came over to the bed, I said to myself:—

"This is she. This is the one for whom I have waited."

She smiled, and a little dimple came in her cheek.

"Ah! I'm glad you've come to your senses again. How do you feel?"

"Perfectly content and happy. I seem to be in a pleasant dream."

"That's good. You've had dreams enough, in the last month, that didn't seem pleasant. You must keep quiet. I'll be back in a minute."

She returned with her mother, who gave me some medicine, and a drink of broth, and I fell asleep. When I awoke, the pretty girl was knitting by the fire. She got me some broth, and after I had drunk it brought a flax wheel and sat down by it. I was sick and weak, but the joy of Michael Wigglesworth's saints in heaven was nothing compared to mine. That is, until the dreadful thought occurred that she might have been already sought and won by someone else. But I said, "Keep your courage up, Ben. She isn't over seventeen. I'm sick, and she's here, and I won't get well in a hurry."

Ruth

How well I remember her, sitting by the flax wheel, spinning,— even the pepper and salt homespun dress, the blue and white checked apron, the little shoes with the silver buckles, and the glimpse of gray stocking.

"Will you please tell me your name?"

"Ruth. Ruth Elliot."

"Ruth? That's the sweetest name of all. It suits you too. But where am I, and what good fortune brought me here?"

"You are at Fort No. 4, or Charlestown as they call it now. You were with Rogers in the woods, and floated down the river with Sergeant Munro and Amos Locke. You have been out of your head with a fever for nearly a month."

"Yes, yes. I remember now. How many of the Rangers got back?"

"About one hundred. They came in at different places. Twelve days after you arrived, Rogers came down with those who were at the Ammonusuc. Some were insane, and some had died before he reached them. It was good to see them back again. But they were terribly wasted and worn. After they had been here a few days, they started for Crown Point, over the road which Captain Stark has just cut through the woods."

"One hundred out of one hundred and forty-five? Well, it might have been worse. And what news is there of General Wolfe and his army? When I last heard of them, they were on their way up the St. Lawrence to Quebec."

"Quebec is taken."

"That's good. General Wolfe will get great praise and reward for that."

"If he were alive, he might, but there was a desperate fight, and Wolfe was killed in it, and Montcalm too."

"Both dead? They were brave men and skillful soldiers. Cut off in their prime like Lord Howe. And what is Amherst doing?"

Ben Tells His Adventures

"Amherst is rebuilding the fort at Crown Point. He will do nothing more this year. It is too late. In the spring he will go down and take Montreal, and end the war."

"And the Rangers—what about them?"

"Most of them have gone home. Sergeant Munro and Mr. Locke passed through here a few days ago. They would have stopped, but the fort is full of sick soldiers, and as they could be of no help, they went on their way."

When she had given me the news, it was her turn to question, and mine to answer. I had to tell her all of our adventures during the war, and she laughed and cried over them. I grew more and more deeply in love. I was in no haste to get well, but nature was against me. Every bit of food she gave me seemed to have some wonderful life-giving power in it and my health came back in bounds. After it returned, I nearly fell sick again from the dreadful fear that I might lose her. As the time for my departure approached, our conversation would halt and stop, and we sat in silence. I felt downhearted and hadn't the courage to test my fate, until one day I saw the tears gather in her eyes and trickle down her cheeks. Then we soon had an understanding, and our lightheartedness came back.

"Oh, Ben, I couldn't bear to have you leave, and now I'm so happy."

But she was a willful thing, and though her name was Ruth, she objected to following the example of her namesake in the Bible.

"I may be Ruth, but you're not Boaz."

I stoutly asserted that I was baptized Benjamin Boaz Comee, but I could not bring her to see that she should leave all and follow me.

"No, no, Benjamin Boaz. You're a pretender, and times have changed. I might not like your people, and they might not like me. Father thinks a deal of you, and mother loves you as if you were her own son. And you repay their love by trying to steal me away from them. Is that fair to them, Boaz? Don't you think they would miss their little girl? And that their life would be gloomy without me? And besides, Ben, you told me that they had all the blacksmiths in Lexington that were needed, and that your chances would be poor. And here we're just pining for another blacksmith. The new road through the woods puts us on the main highway to Canada, and there's no better place for a blacksmith than this.

Now that the Indians are gone, you could take up some of that intervale land up the river, that they talk about, and then I'm here, and if Benjamin Boaz Comee wants Ruth, he must follow her. Ben, I like my own way."

Wanted: A Blacksmith

"I like your own way too, and will live wherever you please, provided it be with you."

I returned home, and found Amos telling Davy of our adventures. For a time Davy had little to say about his hunting stories.

I went back to No. 4, opened a blacksmith's shop, and in the fall married Ruth. We have lived here ever since, and have prospered. Much of my success is due to my wife's clear head and wonderful common sense. Folks regard Colonel Comee as a very shrewd and able business man. But my friends laugh, and say:—

"Colonel Ben's just a figure-head. He never takes an important step without talking it over with Aunt Ruth."

John Stark and I have always remained close friends. When he was a colonel at Bunker's Hill, I was a lieutenant in his regiment, and served under him throughout the Revolution. He became a general, and showed the ability that we recognized in the French War.

By the end of the Revolution I had risen to the rank of colonel. Hardly a year has passed since that time that one of us has not made the other a visit of a few days. He has always retained a great admiration and tender affection for Lord Howe.

After the French War was over, Rogers was appointed to the command of the post at Michilimackinac. His accounts did not come out right. He always had that failing, and he went to England to explain matters. While over there, he was riding one night in a stage-coach over Hounslow Heath, when a masked highwayman stopped the coach, and thrusting his pistols in at the window, told the passengers to hand over their money and watches. They were doing so, when Rogers, who was wonderfully strong, quickly reached out, grabbed the highwayman by the collar of his coat, pulled him into the coach, sat on him, took away his pistols, tied him up, and delivered him over to the authorities. He was an old offender, for whose apprehension a reward of £50 had been offered, which Rogers claimed and received.

A Surprised Highwayman

Rogers remained in England until the Revolution, and then came over here, and after a while offered his services to Washington. He came to Stark's headquarters at Medford, and John and I had a long talk with him.

Stark believed he would be true to us, and so did I. But he had been on such close terms of intimacy with the British that Washington distrusted him and would not give him a command.

Soon after he received a commission from the British, and raised the Queen's Rangers, who were badly defeated in a fight in Connecticut.

Rogers then returned to England, and led a rather shady life; and I believe was finally killed while fighting in Algiers. He was a curious compound. If he had only been a man of honor, he would have become a great man. But his tricky, unscrupulous nature was his ruin.

Edmund Munro served again at Crown Point in 1762-63, as a lieutenant, and as adjutant of the four provincial regiments stationed there.

I met him often in the Revolution. He was captain of the Lexington company. Poor fellow, he was killed by a cannon ball at Monmouth, at the head of his company. He died poor, and his widow had a hard time until the little ones grew up.

Of our old playmate, John Hancock, you have all heard, how he inherited the wealth of his Uncle Thomas, and in his turn was the richest man in Boston, and lived in the stone house on Beacon Hill.

You remember how he risked his great fortune and his head, and sided with his countrymen. His bold signature heads the signers of the Declaration of Independence. Riches and honors came to him. Year after year he was chosen governor of Massachusetts.

Governor Hancock

I did not meet him from the time I went to the French War until some ten years after the Revolution.

I called on him in Boston, and he was glad to see me, and had me up to his house to lunch and to spend the night.

Everything was magnificent. John was kind, but condescending—something like a great mogul receiving an inferior.

I had no favor to ask of him. I saw no reason why I should look up to and revere him. I had played my own part in life well and boldly and stood firm on my feet. When John found I was not in awe of his rank and magnificence, he gave up his grand airs and was again the bright, lively fellow I knew as a boy.

Hector and Donald Munro remained in this country. After the French War was over, they visited their kinsmen in Lexington, and then went to Rehoboth, where there is another branch of the family, and settled in that town.

My old wrestling-master, Jonas Parker, was killed on the common at Lexington, on the 19th of April, 1775. He had said in his grim way, "Some may run from the British, but I won't budge a foot."

He was in the front rank of the minutemen. He laid his hat on the ground before him, and in it placed his powder-horn and bullets.

When the British fired, he was wounded, and fell to his knees. He returned their fire, and was reloading, when the regulars ran forward and killed him with their bayonets.

Amos and Davy were in the Revolution, too. They never got over their love for fox hunting and pigeon-shooting.

As I finish this record, sixty years have passed since we had the pigeon shoot on Bull Meadow Hill. Those of us who survive are old, but some of us are still hale and hearty.

Amos Has a Story, Too

I received a letter the other day from a friend in Lexington, in which he says:—

"About a week ago I saw your old friend, Amos Locke, ploughing in a field which joins on to my farm. I walked over to the wall. When he saw me, he left his plough, came to the wall, and said,—

"'Morning! M-mighty good day to go after p-pigeons. P-Puts me in mind of the d-day I was with Weaver David and B-Ben Comee, up on Bull Meadow Hill, and shot fifty-two p-pigeons at one shot. One for every week in the year. I'll t-tell you about it.'"

Recommended Books

The challenge, the pain and the leadership value of U. S. Army Ranger School have been squeezed into the pages of this book. Experience the first book to illuminate the best leadership school in the U.S. Army; Ranger School. Ranger School puts you at ground level and drives home leadership principles through impactful first-person stories. Learn what Ranger School is like. Feel the claustrophobia of the first night, the frustration of exhaustion and the pain of hunger. This is the perfect in-depth source for tab seekers and for anyone wishing to know how to become someone worthy of being followed. Graduates will be reunited with their own extraordinary experiences and determination. Leaders don't make excuses!

The Art of War Organized for Decision Making. A Must Have Resource for Every Art of War Enthusiast. Strategic planning with The Art of War is now possible. The effective application of Sun Tzu's Art of War was a guessing game prior to this organization of the book. Brace Barber discarded proverbs meaningless to modern society in order to focus the reader, eliminate distraction and allow for clear strategic thinking. He then reorganized the Art of War in line with accepted strategic categories necessary for systematically analyzing a problem and developing a highly stable course of action. This book is your key to an advanced strategic IQ.

Printed in Great Britain
by Amazon